FACTS AT YOUR FINGERTIPS

WAR ON
TERROR

FACTS AT YOUR FINGERTIPS

WAR ON
TERROR

BROWN
BEAR
BOOKS

Published by Brown Bear Books

An imprint of
The Brown Reference Group Ltd
68 Topstone Road
Redding
Connecticut
06896
USA

www.brownreference.com

Library of Congress Cataloging-in-Publication Data
available upon request.

ISBN-13 978-1-933834-53-5

Author: Steve Crawford
Editorial Director: Lindsey Lowe
Senior Managing Editor: Tim Cooke
Designer: Sarah Williams
Maps: Darren Awuah
Picture researcher: Andrew Webb
Editor: Peter Darman

Printed in the United States of America

PICTURE CREDITS

Cover Images
Front: U.S. Navy SEALs hunting terrorists in Latin
America (Corbis/Leif Skoogfers)

Back: U.S. troops and helicopters in Iraq in 2006
(U.S. Department of Defense)

Page 3: U.S. soldiers detonate explosives during
a training exercise in Djibouti, Africa, as part
of "Operation Enduring Freedom" in 2004
(U.S. Department of Defense)

Corbis: epa/Adel Karroum: 47; epa/Peter
Macdiarmid: 26/27; epa/Syed Jan Sabawoon: 12;
epa/Wael Hamzah: 42; Patrick Robert: 11; **Reuters:**
10, 32, 51; **Reuters/Akram Saleh:** 37r;
Reuters/Antony Njuguna: 20l; **Reuters/Dadang Tri:**
52; **Reuters/Faisal Mahmood:** 30; **Reuters/Jayanta
Shaw:** 33; **Reuters/Kai Pfaffenbach:** 26l;
Reuters/Romeo Ranoco: 48; **Roger Ressmeyer:** 58;
Sygma/Alain Nogues: 53; **U.S. Department of
Defense:** 6, 20r, 21, 22, 24/25, 28, 37l, 41, 50, 56, 57;
NATO: 8, 60; **PA Photos:** AP/Peter Lauth: 44;
Shutterstock: Amanda Haddox: 54; **Cristina Ciochina:**
59; **Philip Lange:** 61; **U.S. Army:** 16, 18, 34, 40, 62

CONTENTS

Islam, in principle, is both a religious faith and a political community that includes all Muslims. In modern times, this is not the reality of life for most Muslims, but from an Islamist point of view this is the ideal: one Islamic nation (umma) ruled by its Islamic law ("*sharia*"). The confluence of Islam and politics is not just a characteristic of Islamists. Even among Arab regimes that are not Islamist, the close connection between Islam and politics is common: every political move has a religious Islamic connotation.

While the ideal of Islamic unity is central to all believing Muslims, Islam is, and has been from its early history, divided between two bitterly antagonistic branches: Sunni and Shi'a. The great majority of Muslims in the world (some 90 percent) are Sunnis. In the Middle East, however, the Sunni majority is not so overwhelming. The Shi'as have an important presence not only in Iran and Iraq (which are mostly Shi'a), but also in a number of Arab countries: in Lebanon, where they are probably the largest community; in Saudi Arabia, where their true numbers are kept a state secret; and in the Persian Gulf states.

Iran and Saudi Arabia

The deep rivalry between two critical regional powers—Iran and Saudi Arabia—has a distinct religious dimension. This aspect of the rivalry was less significant prior to the 1979 Islamic Revolution in Iran, when the Shah was nonreligious and both countries were within the U.S. sphere of influence. However, with the Islamic Revolution, things changed dramatically.

The storming of the U.S. Embassy and the taking of U.S. hostages by Iranian students on November 4, 1979, was greeted throughout the Muslim world as a victory for Islam over "infidels" or nonbelievers. These Iranian students—one of whom is believed to have been future Iranian prime minister Ahmadinejad—managed to humiliate the great American superpower. This was a confirmation of an Islamist belief that by acting fearlessly in the name of Islam, Muslims could defeat the enemy. The fact that the victors were Shi'as, a minority group within the Islamic world, did not detract from a great sense of achievement among Muslims in general. In the broader division of the world into two

Saudi-born Osama bin Laden, leader of the terrorist alliance known as al Qaeda (meaning "the base"). Al Qaeda was responsible for the September 11, 2001, attacks which sparked the war on terror.

camps—believers and nonbelievers—there was a near-universal Muslim solidarity with Ayatollah Khomeini's new regime in Iran.

For the Saudi regime, however, the prestige earned by the Islamic Revolution in Iran posed a problem. In their view, it is the House of Saud, the Defender of the Two Holy Places (Mecca and Medina), that is the rightful guardian of true Islam—that is, Sunni Islam, in accordance with Wahhabi doctrine. In their view, it was they who deserved to lead the Islamic awakening, not the heretical Shi'a Ayatollah Khomeini. The religious authority of the House of Saud was a political asset in the pan-Arab and international arena, and even more so within its own kingdom. To preserve their religious status, the Saudis had to win the struggle for primacy as the champions of Islam throughout the world. This was a struggle for the hearts and minds of all Muslims.

Therefore, in response to the challenge posed by the Iranian Revolution, the Saudis took a dual course of action. They embarked on a Jihad (holy war) against the 1979 Soviet invasion of Afghanistan; and they launched a far-reaching operation for the propagation of Islam, investing billions of dollars through Islamic charities to build mosques and religious seminaries (madrasas) across the world. These madrasas and mosques were potential vehicles for the propagation of Jihadi Islam.

The 1989 Soviet defeat in Afghanistan was a great victory for Islamism. A decade after Khomeini's Islamic Shi'a revolution in Iran, Sunni Islam triumphed over the infidel communist power. The United States believed at the time that it had effectively manipulated Islam to deal a blow to the Soviets. Yet, for some Islamists, this was only a single battle in a global drama that would unfold until the ultimate victory of Islam, which would include the defeat of the United States of America. And the tool for this would be al Qaeda.

Al Qaeda is an international terrorist network led by the Saudi Osama bin Laden. It seeks to rid Muslim countries of what it sees as the profane influence of the West and replace their governments with Islamic regimes.

The turning point of 9/11

The next major Islamist "victory" was the attacks on New York City and Washington, D.C., on September 11, 2001, in which 3,000 people died. This was a historic turning point for the entire world, but even more so for the Middle East. It made clear that Islamism is a major factor in the politics of the region in the 21st century. This is something that many Westerners find difficult to fully understand. To be sure, ever since 9/11, Westerners have learned far more about Islamist terrorism. Some people believe that Islamist fanatics are ready to perpetrate any atrocity for the sake of Allah. Others argue that Islamism is a perversion of the principles of Islam.

Immediately after the 9/11 attacks, U.S. President George W. Bush declared a "war on terror" against those who had led them. There followed U.S.-led invasions of Afghanistan and Iraq, which were initially militarily successful. But al Qaeda, as befitting an organization that believes that God is on its side, proved resilient. The War on Terror became a long, drawn-out conflict spread across the globe.

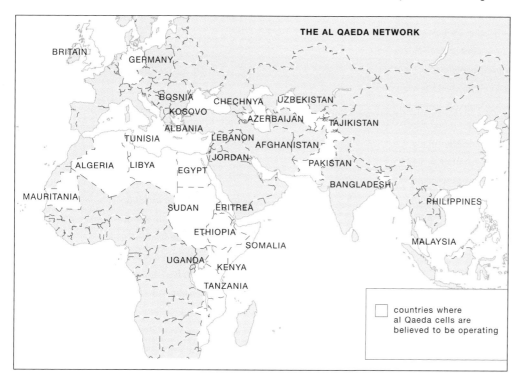

THE AL QAEDA NETWORK

BRITAIN
GERMANY
BOSNIA
KOSOVO
CHECHNYA
UZBEKISTAN
AZERBAIJAN
TAJIKISTAN
ALBANIA
TUNISIA
LEBANON
AFGHANISTAN
JORDAN
PAKISTAN
ALGERIA
LIBYA
EGYPT
BANGLADESH
MAURITANIA
SUDAN
ERITREA
PHILIPPINES
ETHIOPIA
SOMALIA
MALAYSIA
UGANDA
KENYA
TANZANIA

countries where al Qaeda cells are believed to be operating

Al Qaeda cells may remain active for years or engage only in peaceful Islamic activities. However, a cell may suddenly be called into action.

After al Qaeda's September 11, 2001, attacks, the United States launched a war in Afghanistan to destroy al Qaeda's bases there and overthrow the Taliban, the country's fundamentalist Muslim rulers who harbored bin Laden and his followers. The initial military campaign, with the Americans cooperating with local anti-Taliban forces known as the Northern Alliance, went well. The Taliban was removed from power and a pro-Western government was installed in the capital, Kabul. The Taliban was apparently defeated and Afghanistan could be rebuilt to become a pro-Western ally.

To escape the U.S.-led war in Afghanistan, al Qaeda's leadership sought refuge across the border in Pakistan's tribal areas. Bin Laden, along with some other members of the organization, is currently thought to be hiding in Pakistan along the Afghan border. Bin Laden's group is now training most of the terrorist groups in Pakistan's tribal areas.

NATO in Afghanistan

As part of the War on Terror, the United States was assisted in Afghanistan by other members of the North Atlantic Treaty Organization (NATO). Since September 11, 2001, the allies have sought to create a "new" NATO, able to go beyond the European theater of operations to combat new threats, such as terrorism and the proliferation of weapons of mass destruction. Afghanistan is NATO's first "out of area" mission beyond Europe. The purpose of the mission is the stabilization and reconstruction of Afghanistan.

The mission is a supremely difficult one, because it must take place while combat operations against Taliban insurgents continue. Seven years after the U.S. invasion, assessments of the situation in Afghanistan pointed to a rise in the overall level of violence due to increased Taliban military activity and an increase in terrorist-related activities, including suicide bombings.

United Nations (UN) Security Council resolutions govern NATO's responsibilities in Afghanistan. The NATO-led International Security Assistance Force (ISAF)

French soldiers on patrol in Afghanistan as part of NATO's International Security Assistance Force.

faces formidable obstacles: shoring up a weak government in Kabul; using military capabilities in a distant country with rugged terrain; and also rebuilding a country devastated by war and troubled by a resilient narcotics trade. NATO's mission statement lays out the essential elements of the task of stabilizing and rebuilding the country. The main aims are: to train the Afghan army, police, and judiciary; to support the new government in its ongoing antinarcotics operations; to develop a market infrastructure; and to suppress the Taliban.

ISAF has proceeded in four stages to extend its area of responsibility over the whole of Afghanistan. Although the allies agree on ISAF's mission goals, they continue to differ on how to accomplish them. Some allies do not want their forces to engage in counter-insurgency operations. Until recently, only the United States wanted to engage directly in the destruction of poppy fields and drug facilities in attempts to destroy the illegal drug trade. The principal mechanism to rebuild Afghanistan is the Provincial Reconstruction Team (PRT). PRTs, composed of military and civilian officials, are charged with extending the reach of the Afghan government by improving governance and rebuilding the economy. There are, however, significant differences in how individual NATO governments operate their PRTs. Increasing turmoil in Pakistan has also complicated efforts to prevent the Taliban from infiltrating Afghanistan.

Talking to the Taliban?

By 2008, it appeared that NATO's military effort in Afghanistan was failing. Violence in and around Kabul reached record highs, corruption is rampant, and pessimism rose. A U.S. intelligence assessment of the situation said Afghanistan was in a "downward spiral," fueled by drug money and a weak central government. Brigadier Mark Carleton-Smith, commander of British forces, stated on October 6, 2008, that a military victory in Afghanistan is "neither feasible nor supportable." It appeared that the only solution to the war in Afghanistan was a negotiated settlement with the Taliban, something that the Americans in particular did not relish.

BATTLE FOR MAZAR-I-SHARIF

Until Northern Alliance troops finally closed in on Mazar-i-Sharif, with the help of U.S. Special Forces and air support, the war had yielded no major successes to help sustain political support for combat operations in Afghanistan. Mazar-i-Sharif is the most important city in northern Afghanistan, with two airports and a road link to Uzbekistan. Controlling these would give Northern Alliance and American forces a forward base inside Afghanistan and a useful military resupply route. The Northern Alliance attacked the city on November 9, and, within two days, Taliban forces were fleeing south.

Triumphant Northern Alliance troops enter the Afghan capital, Kabul, atop a Russian T-62 tank on November 13, 2001.

BATTLE FOR MAZAR-I-SHARIF

Location Mazar-i-Sharif, Afghanistan

Date November 9, 2001

Commanders and forces Taliban: 10,000 troops; Northern Alliance: 40,000 troops (General Abdul Rashid Dostum)

Casualties Taliban: 90 killed, 500 taken prisoner; Northern Alliance: 12 killed and wounded

Key actions On November 9, U.S. aircraft bombed Taliban defenders concentrated in the Chesmay-e-Safa gorge that marked the southern entrance to the city. The use of massive air power was decisive in the battle. At 14:00 hours, Northern Alliance forces attacked from the south and west, seizing the city's main military base and airport.

Key effects The capture of Mazar-i-Sharif provided an important military, psychological and political boost to the U.S.-led campaign to drive the Taliban from power and to bring Osama bin Laden to justice.

THE FALL OF KABUL

After the fall of Mazar-i-Sharif, Northern Alliance forces rushed south toward Kabul. The U.S. had pressed for the Alliance to stay out of Kabul to allow time for a coalition government including members of the southern-based Pashtun tribe to be formed. While some Taliban fled before the city was abandoned, others engaged the Alliance on the Shomali plain about 25 miles (40 km) north of the capital.

Taliban soldiers and their allies—Arabs, Pakistanis, Chechens, and others—were rushed up to block the Alliance's advance into Kabul. The Taliban ringed the city with tanks. In four days, the Northern Alliance had expanded its territory from 10 percent of Afghanistan to more than 40 percent. The country was now effectively partitioned, with the Alliance in control of the north and the Taliban dug in in the south. The Alliance troops encountered little resistance as they emerged from their

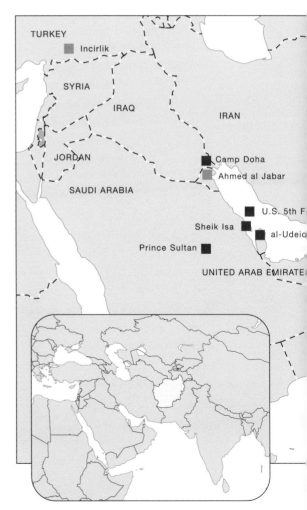

positions at Bagram, north of Kabul, and marched across no-man's land. U.S. and British troops advanced with Northern Alliance fighters and called in air strikes against Taliban positions. The Taliban abandoned their positions as trucks loaded with heavily armed Alliance soldiers were seen moving unopposed into Kabul.

THE FALL OF KABUL

Location   Afghanistan

Date   November 13, 2001

Commanders and forces   Taliban: 10,000 troops; Northern Alliance: 40,000 troops (General Abdul Rashid Dostum)

Casualties   Taliban: 20 killed; Northern Alliance: none

Key effects   Within 12 hours of the fall of Kabul, the Northern Alliance foreign minister said his group was ready to share political power. The UN Special Envoy for Afghanistan met with the Security Council in New York and proposed establishing a multinational security force and a plan for a transitional government to run the country.

AIR BASES AT DISPOSAL OF UN FOR
OPERATIONS IN AFGHANISTAN

REPORTED BASE

KNOWN BASE

POTENTIAL BASE

THE FALL OF KUNDUZ

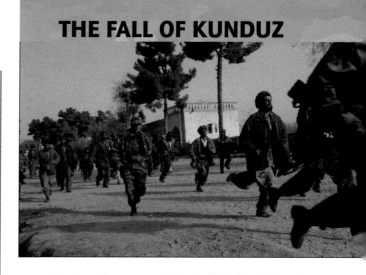

Northern Alliance troops take Kunduz, Afghanistan, in November 2001. This was the Taliban's last stronghold in the north.

The capture of Kunduz came hours after Alliance troops gained a foothold inside the besieged city, then overran a town on its eastern flank. Near the town of Khanabad, 10 miles (16 km) east of Kunduz, Alliance troops spread across ridgetops held by the Taliban a day earlier and fanned out across fields to check mud buildings for enemy fighters. Over the previous three weeks, the Taliban had lost most of their territory and the capital, Kabul. Kunduz was defended by Taliban and foreign fighters, some loyal to Osama bin Laden.

Many of the foreign Taliban fighters were secretly evacuated from the city by Pakistani aircraft. This act outraged Northern Alliance commanders, but the U.S. government in Washington, D.C., was deeply indebted to the Islamabad government for supporting its war against the Taliban. Although it said it wanted all the foreign fighters trapped in Kunduz captured, it decided for diplomatic reasons not to protest the airlift.

THE FALL OF KUNDUZ

Location   Kunduz, Afghanistan

Date   November 12–25, 2001

Commanders and forces   Taliban: 10,000 plus 3,000 foreign fighters; Northern Alliance: 40,000 (General Daoud Khan)

Casualties   Taliban: 5,000 taken prisoner; Northern Alliance: unknown

Key actions   As Northern Alliance troops prepared to enter Kunduz on November 25, fears that the city's fall might result in a massacre of foreign-born Taliban fighters were averted by a secret deal hatched between Pakistan and Northern Alliance commanders, with Washington's compliance, to fly the foreigners out of the city using Pakistani aircraft.

Key effects   The fall of Kunduz marked the loss of the Taliban's last garrison in the north of Afghanistan, leaving the Islamic militia with a stronghold only in the southern city of Kandahar.

THE CAPTURE OF KANDAHAR

BATTLE OF TORA BORA

By the end of November, Kandahar was the last Taliban stronghold and was under increasing pressure. Nearly 3,000 tribal fighters, led by Hamid Karzai and Gul Agha Sherzai, put pressure on Taliban forces from the east and cut off the northern Taliban supply lines to the town. The threat of the Northern Alliance loomed in the north and northeast. Meanwhile, the first significant U.S. combat troops had arrived. Nearly 1,000 Marines set up "Camp Rhino" in the desert south of Kandahar on November 25. This was the Coalition's first strategic foothold within Afghanistan. The first significant combat involving U.S. ground forces then occurred on November 26, when 15 armored vehicles approached Camp Rhino and were attacked by U.S. helicopter gunships, which destroyed many of them.

A British soldier of the NATO-led International Security Force patrols in Kabul, the Afghan capital, in July 2006.

Tora Bora is a cave complex situated in the White Mountains of eastern Afghanistan, near the Khyber Pass. The whole area is riddled with cave and tunnel complexes that are ancient in origin, but which had been further excavated and developed by Afghan and Arab fighters during their struggle against the Soviet Army in the 1980s, following the USSR's invasion of Afghanistan in 1979. The complex was thought to use hydroelectric power generated by mountain streams and to be capable of sheltering around 1,000 people. Further, it was suspected that caches of ammunition, such as missiles left over from the war with the Soviet Union, were stored there.

In early December 2001, the American Central Intelligence Agency (CIA) believed that al Qaeda leader Osama bin Laden and close to 1,000 Taliban and al Qaeda fighters had made their way to Tora Bora and were firmly established there in strongly defended positions. The attack against the Tora Bora complex was conducted mainly by Afghan forces, with only six U.S. Green Beret troops accompanying them on the ground. However, the U.S. Air Force provided round-the-clock air support.

A turning point came on December 12, when Haji Zaman, one of the Afghan commanders leading the attack, opened negotiations with members of al Qaeda. These talks resulted in many al Qaeda troops, including Osama Bin Laden, being allowed to escape west into Pakistan. By December 17, the cave complex had been captured and the remaining defenders killed.

THE CAPTURE OF KANDAHAR

Location   Kandahar, Afghanistan

Date   November 25–December 7, 2001

Commanders and forces   Taliban: 12,000 troops (Mullah Mohammed Omar); Afghan tribes: led by Gul Agha; U.S.: 1,300 Marines

Casualties   unknown

Key actions   Once again, the U.S. aerial bombardment turned out to be highly effective. On December 8, U.S. Marines attacked Taliban troops fleeing the southern city, as the hunt for Mullah Omar intensified. The attack took place when Marines in heavily armed, light-armored vehicles, who were deployed to block Taliban and al Qaeda supply and escape routes, killed seven people and destroyed three vehicles. One carrier-based F/A-18 fighter-bomber aircraft also joined the strike.

Key effects   Taliban rule in Afghanistan had collapsed, but they retained the ability to wage a guerrilla war.

BATTLE OF TORA BORA

Location   Nangarhar Province, Afghanistan

Date   December 3–17, 2001

Commanders and forces   Taliban and al Qaeda: 1,000 fighters (Osama bin Laden); Northern Alliance: unknown; U.S.: Special Forces

Casualties   Taliban: 200 killed; Northern Alliance: unknown

Key actions   The Tora Bora operation failed for two reasons. First, the warlords and the narcotics barons played a double game. While ostensibly helping the U.S. forces, they kept Osama bin Laden and his fighters informed of U.S. military movements. Second, Pakistan, on which the United States depended for sealing off its border with Afghanistan to prevent the escape of bin Laden and other jihadi terrorists into Pakistani territory, quietly let them pass.

Key effects   Al Qaeda forces began regrouping in the Shah-i-Kot mountains of Paktia Province throughout January and February 2002.

OPERATION ANACONDA

AFGHANISTAN

Kabul River

Jalalabad

Lalpur

Garikhil · · Mileva

TORA BORA

PAKTIA
PROVINCE

Gardez

Khost

KHOST
PROVINCE

KITKA
OVINCE

PAKISTAN

THE LOCATION OF THE TORA BORA CAVE COMPLEX

AFGHANISTAN

Following the Tora Bora battles, indications grew that there was a major concentration of enemy forces in the Shah-i-Kot Valley nearby. The Alliance attempt to deal with this enemy force was codenamed "Operation Anaconda." The Alliance attacked a concentration of al Qaeda and Taliban fighters south of Gardez in eastern Afghanistan. The aircraft flying daily missions over the battlefield (10 long-range bombers, 30 to 40 fighters, and 2 to 4 AC-130 gunships) were more than double the size of the force used in strikes across Afghanistan in the fall of 2001. More than 350 bombs and missiles were dropped during the first four days of fighting in support of Afghan, U.S., and Coalition forces. By March 5, 2002, over 450 bombs had been dropped. In response, the Taliban managed to put up some token resistance, and a few U.S. Army AH-64 Apache attack helicopters were hit by enemy fire. However, by the end of March, nearly 3,500 bombs had been dropped.

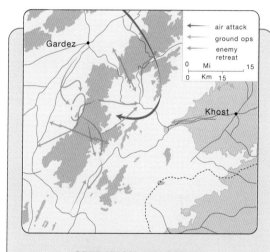

OPERATION ANACONDA

Location Shah-i-Kot Valley, Paktia Province, Afghanistan

Date March 1–18, 2002

Commanders and forces Al Qaeda and Taliban: 1,000 troops; Afghan Government: 1,000 militia; U.S.: 10th Mountain Division, the 101st Airborne Division, 160th Special Operations Aviation Regiment, and Special Operations forces (Major General Franklin L. Hagenbeck, 1,700 troops)

Casualties Al Qaeda and Taliban: 500 killed; U.S.: 8 killed, 82 wounded

Key actions U.S. aircraft dropped 190 bombs on Sunday, March 3, 2002, more than twice as many as on the previous day.

Key effects "Anaconda" was the last opportunity to kill off al Qaeda troops in a large group. The opportunity was in part squandered—less by the officers on the ground in Afghanistan than by their leaders in the Pentagon and at Central Command (Centcom).

THE TALIBAN FIGHTS BACK

Between 2003 and 2005, the Taliban began to fight back against U.S. and NATO forces in Afghanistan. The United States had managed to defeat the Taliban with apparent ease in 2001–2002, partly by employing air power and special forces, but primarily by boosting the Northern Alliance. However, in most parts of Taliban-controlled Afghanistan, when faced with U.S.-led advances, Taliban groups simply melted away to towns and villages on both sides of the Afghanistan–Pakistan border. They often kept their weapons intact, yet the militants and their supplies were so dispersed that there was little possibility of identifying either.

In addition, after the Taliban's fall from power, the United States and its coalition partners failed to provide sufficient security assistance to the new Afghan government under the leadership of Hamid Karzai. United Nations' specialists estimated that the coalition would need at least 30,000 troops to create stability in the country and to allow development programs to take hold. However, barely a third of this number was actually provided. There was also an increase in anti-Americanism in some sectors of Afghan society, especially when U.S. combat forces used large-scale firepower to subdue local militias. By the end of 2005, the Taliban still had an estimated 12,000 fighters within Afghanistan and entrenched in the border regions of western Pakistan.

COMMAND STRUCTURE IN AFGHANISTAN

Combined Joint Task Force 180 (CJTF-180) was formed in June 2002 as the forward headquarters in Afghanistan, commanded by a lieutenant general. Leadership of CJTF-180 changed in mid-April 2004 to the U.S. 25th Infantry Division (Light), resulting in a designator change to CJTF-76. The Southern European Task Force (SETAF) took control of CJTF-76 in March 2005 and the U.S. 10th Mountain Division (Light) again took command of CJTF-76 in February 2006, neither of which resulted in a designator change. The mission of CJTF within Afghanistan continued to be to conduct full-spectrum operations intended to prevent the re-emergence of terror organizations and to set the conditions for the growth of democracy in Afghanistan.

In March 2007, the U.S. 82nd Airborne Division took control of the CJTF in Afghanistan, resulting in a designator change to CJTF-82. In addition to the previous responsibilities, the commander of CJTF-82, a major general, was also placed in charge of U.S. forces detailed to the NATO International Stabilization Assistance Force (ISAF) in Afghanistan, and assumed the role of commander of ISAF Regional Command East. In April 2008, the U.S. 101st Airborne Division (Air Assault) took over control of the CJTF in Afghanistan from the 82nd Airborne Division, resulting in a designator change to CJTF-101.

NATO IN AFGHANISTAN

From January 2006, a NATO International Security Assistance Force (ISAF) force began to replace U.S troops in southern Afghanistan. The British 16th Air Assault Brigade was the core of the force, along with troops from Australia, Canada, and the Netherlands. "Operation Mountain Thrust" was launched on May 17, 2006, to root out Taliban forces. Canadian troops were at the forefront of the fighting during the first major battle at Panjwaii. More than 1,100 Taliban fighters were killed and 400 captured in the six-week operation.

In July 2006, NATO forces under British General David J. Richards took over. "Operation Medusa" was then launched and the Second Battle of Panjwaii saw 500 Taliban fighters killed. Also in 2006, 5,000 British troops were deployed to Helmand Province, where they and Canadian forces encountered very fierce fighting through the rest of 2006. Although NATO achieved some tactical victories, the Taliban were not defeated and NATO had to continue operations into 2007.

COUNTRIES CONTRIBUTING FORCES TO AFGHANISTAN

By the end of 2006, the following countries had sent troops to support the NATO effort in Afghanistan:

Country	Number of troops	Country	Number of troops
Albania	30	Latvia	30
Australia	200	Lithuania	140
Austria	5	Luxemburg	10
Azerbaijan	20	Netherlands	2,000
Belgium	340	New Zealand	100
Bulgaria	150	Iceland	15
Canada	2,500	Norway	320
Croatia	100	Poland	160
Czech Republic	100	Portugal	150
Denmark	300	Romania	750
Estonia	90	Slovakia	60
Finland	90	Slovenia	50
France	975	Spain	650
Macedonia	120	Sweden	200
Germany	2,700	Switzerland	5
Greece	170	Turkey	460
Hungary	200	UK	6,000
Ireland	10	USA	11,800
Italy	1,800	**Total**	**32,800**

NATO forces continued to fight the Taliban in 2007 and 2008 in a war that showed no signs of ending. In January and February 2007, British Royal Marines mounted "Operation Volcano" to clear insurgents from the village of Barikju, north of Kajaki. This was followed by "Operation Achilles," a major offensive from March to late May. Further operations, such as "Operation Silver" and "Operation Silicon," were conducted to keep the pressure on the Taliban. On March 4, 2007, at least 12 civilians were killed and 33 injured by U.S. Marines in the Shinwar district of the Nangrahar Province. The event became known as the Shinwar Massacre.

On August 28, 2007, 100 Taliban fighters were killed in the Shah Wali Kot district of Kandahar Province. On October 28, 2007, about 80 Taliban fighters were killed in a six-hour battle with forces from the U.S.-led coalition in Afghanistan's Helmand Province. During the last days of October, Canadian forces killed 50 Taliban fighters near Arghandab. In addition, security operations were conducted in the north by ISAF and Afghan forces, including "Operation Harekate Yolo I & II."

The Taliban continued to attack Afghan government and coalition bases in 2008. On June 13, they freed all 1,200 prisoners from Kandahar jail, 400 of whom were Taliban prisoners of war. On September 3, the war spilled over into Pakistani territory for the first time, when units of heavily armed U.S. special forces landed by helicopter and attacked three houses in a village close to a known Taliban and al Qaeda stronghold.

As 2008 came toward an end, the security of Afghanistan and its economic development were still hampered by a sharp increase in poppy cultivation and drug trafficking. In addition, Afghan relations with Pakistan continued to be strained, as Taliban and Pashtun militants continued to operate in Afghanistan from havens across the Pakistan border.

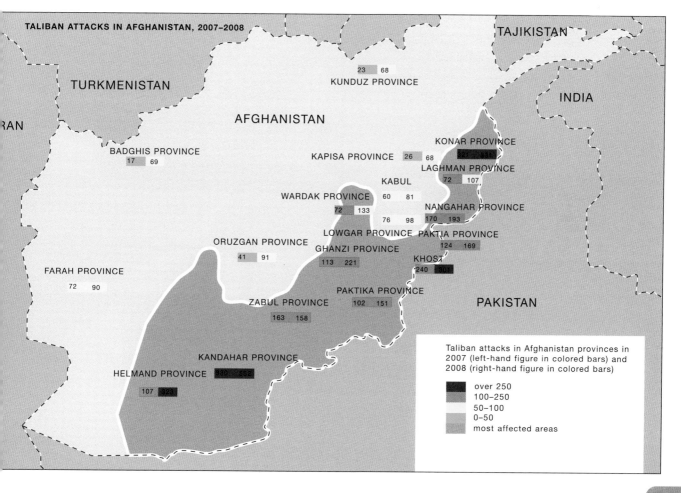

TALIBAN ATTACKS IN AFGHANISTAN, 2007–2008

TURKMENISTAN

TAJIKISTAN

INDIA

AFGHANISTAN

KUNDUZ PROVINCE — 23 68

KONAR PROVINCE

BADGHIS PROVINCE — 17 69

KAPISA PROVINCE — 26 68

LAGHMAN PROVINCE — 72 107

KABUL — 60 81

WARDAK PROVINCE — 72 133

NANGAHAR PROVINCE — 170 193

76 98

LOWGAR PROVINCE

ORUZGAN PROVINCE — 41 91

GHANZI PROVINCE — 113 221

PAKTIA PROVINCE — 124 169

KHOST — 240 301

FARAH PROVINCE — 72 90

PAKTIKA PROVINCE — 102 151

PAKISTAN

ZABUL PROVINCE — 163 158

KANDAHAR PROVINCE

HELMAND PROVINCE — 330 552 / 107 423

Taliban attacks in Afghanistan provinces in 2007 (left-hand figure in colored bars) and 2008 (right-hand figure in colored bars)

- over 250
- 100–250
- 50–100
- 0–50
- most affected areas

In **the first** decade of the 21st century, the U.S. military embarked on a long-term push into Africa to counter what it considered growing inroads by al Qaeda and other terrorist networks in poor, lawless, and predominantly Muslim expanses of the continent.

The Pentagon planned to train thousands of African troops in battalions equipped for extended desert and border operations and to link the militaries of different countries with satellite communications. The initiative covered Algeria, Chad, Mali, Mauritania, Niger, Senegal, Nigeria, Morocco, and Tunisia.

The Pentagon also assigned more military officers to U.S. embassies in the region, bolstering the gathering and sharing of intelligence, locating austere landing strips for use in emergencies, and securing greater access and legal protection for U.S. troops through new bilateral agreements.

Terrorism in the Horn of Africa

The thrust into Africa was considered vital to head off infiltration by international terrorist groups. Terrorists were believed to be recruiting hundreds of members in Africa and Europe, attacking local governments and Western interests, and profiting from tribal smuggling routes to obtain arms, cash, and hideouts. Meanwhile, small groups of Islamic radicals were moving into Africa from Iraq, where Africans made up about a quarter of the foreign fighters.

The U.S. government claimed that the Islamic Courts Union in Somalia is "controlled by al Qaeda cell individuals." U.S. strategy toward Somalia was three-pronged: to eliminate the terrorist threat, to promote political stability, and to address the humanitarian crisis. However, Somalia is far more complex than the U.S. or its Ethiopian allies would like to admit. Since 1991 there has been no stable government. In 2004 Kenya, worried by the impact that a politicized brand of Islam in Somalia would have on its own Muslim minority, helped get agreement from various warlords to establish a Transitional Federal Government (TFG). The TRG, itself made up of some very unsavory

A U.S. soldier befriends a group of curious children in Djibouti during a mission to provide force protection for Combined Joint Task Force-Horn of Africa (CJTF-HOA) personnel in March 2004.

characters, initially pretended to "run" Somalia from Kenya, although in fact it actually controlled almost none of the country. Nonetheless it has received international backing, containing as it does so many of the warring factions and tribes.

The Islamic Courts Union was not recognized internationally but had popular support in Somalia and effectively controlled most of the country. Some Somalis praised the stability that it brought after so many years of chaos and violence, but it also appeared to be taking an increasingly hardline position in terms of internal law and order. Indeed, religious forms of justice were widely seen as the only way to rise above warlord violence.

Violence without end

Ethiopia had secretly stationed at least 8,000 troops in Somalia from the Transitional Federal Government capital in Baidoa. In October 2006, the Islamic Courts issued a threat to Ethiopia to leave Somalia. Ethiopia, with backing from the United States, decided it was time to invade its neighbor, conducting air raids, and in 2007 entering the capital Mogadishu, as the Islamic Courts withdrew. The Ethiopian government made its intentions clear: "We are going to use any appropriate means to destabilize the anti-Ethiopian forces in Somalia."

By early 2009, Ethiopia appeared to have won, at least temporarily. The warlords in the Transitional Federal Government were installed as Somalia's de facto government. Ethiopia claimed that 1,000 or 2,000 people were killed in the operation, with 4,000 to 5,000 wounded, while tens of thousands risked being displaced. Martial law was declared to attempt to rein in the chaos that returned to the streets of Mogadishu. But the Transitional Federal Government was highly unstable, unpopular, and broke, while the Islamic Courts seemed highly likely to re-start an insurgency. Countries throughout the Horn of Africa were also effected. Eritrea supported the Islamic Courts while Kenya supported the Transitional Federal Government, while there were religious and ethnic divisions in Sudan. Meanwhile, al Qaeda continued to operate in the region.

Combined Task Force (CTF) 150 was established near the beginning of Operation Enduring Freedom to conduct Maritime Security Operations (MSO) in the Gulf of Aden, Gulf of Oman, Arabian Sea, Red Sea, and Indian Ocean. The aims of MSO are to help develop security in the maritime environment and thus promote stability and global prosperity. Its operations were intended to complement the counterterrorism and security efforts of regional nations and seek to disrupt extremists' use of the maritime environment for violent attacks or to transport personnel and weapons.

Since its inception, CTF 150 has been commanded by military chiefs from France, Netherlands, Britain, Pakistan, and Canada.

U.S. soldiers detonate explosives during a training exercise in Djibouti, Africa, as part of Operation Enduring Freedom in 2004.

COMBINED JOINT TASK FORCE

In October 2002, the United States established the Combined Joint Task Force (CJTF) Horn of Africa (HOA). For the task force, the Horn of Africa was defined as "the total airspace and land areas out to the high-water mark of Kenya, Somalia, Ethiopia, Sudan, Eritrea, Djibouti, and Yemen." The headquarters of the task force was Camp Lemonier, Djibouti.

The mission of the CJTF-HOA is to detect, disrupt, and defeat terrorists who pose an imminent threat to coalition partners in the region. The task force also works with host nations to prevent the reemergence of terrorist cells and their activities by supporting international agencies working to enhance long-term stability in the region.

The main objectives of the CJTF-HOA are the four "P"s:

• PREVENT Conflict

• PROMOTE Regional Cooperation

• PROTECT U.S. and Coalition Interests

• PREVAIL against Extremism

The CJTF-HOA is made up of about 2,000 personnel from each military branch of the U.S. armed forces, as well as civilian employees and representatives of Coalition and partner countries (Djibouti, Ethiopia, Eritrea, Kenya, Uganda, Somalia, Sudan, Tanzania, Yemen, Seychelles, Comoros, Mauritius, and Madagascar).

Al Qaeda in the Islamic Maghreb (AQIM) is the result of al Qaeda's efforts to unite the various Salafist terror groups within North Africa. AQIM is made up of the Algerian-based Salafist Group for Prayer and Combat (GSPC), the Moroccan Islamic Combat Group, the Tunisian Combatant Group, and elements of the Libyan Islamic Fighting Group. The GSPC forms the nucleus of al Qaeda in the Islamic Maghreb. The GSPC officially merged with al Qaeda in September 2006 and renamed the group al Qaeda in the Islamic Maghreb in January 2007.

Terror attacks rose sharply in Algeria after the GSPC focused its energy on attacking government and military institutions. The Algerian government has claimed to make great strides against al Qaeda, with scores of terrorists killed and captured in various raids and operations, but the terrorist group succeeded in pulling off multiple coordinated suicide bombing attacks in Algiers and beyond in 2007. Attacks were conducted against the office of the prime minister, the president of Algeria as he was campaigning, the security services headquarters, a naval barracks, and a number of public marketplaces. In December 2007, the UNHCR office in Algiers was attacked with a suicide car bombing, killing 17 employees.

Al Qaeda then stepped up its terror campaign in Algeria in the summer of 2008. On August 3, a suicide bomber wounded 25 Algerians, including four police officers, in an attack on a police station in the town of Tizi Ouzou. A suicide bomber killed eight Algerians and wounded eight more during an attack on a police station in Zemmouri on August 10. Nine days later, a suicide car bomber killed 43 Algerians and wounded more than 45 in an attack on a police academy in the town of Issers.

AL QAEDA IN AFRICA

The following African organizations have pledged their allegiance to Osama bin Laden, al Qaeda, and their strategic objectives:

Al Qaeda in Levant and Egypt-Abdallah Azzam Brigades (Egypt);

Qaedat-al-Jihad in Yemen, Liwa al-Tawid (Yemen);

Abu-ali al-Harithi Brigades (Yemen);

Al-Qaeda Maghreb Commandment (Morocco).

In 2002, Eritrean President Isaias Afwerki said his country would cooperate in the global war on terrorism, because it had been the victim of terrorism. The failed state of Somalia is near Eritrea, and al Qaeda leader Osama bin Laden was based in adjacent Sudan until 1996. A 1998–2000 border war with Ethiopia disrupted the area and allowed terrorists to operate unhindered. Eritrea, a nation of some 4.9 million people on the Red Sea, also offered facilities, intelligence, and other help to the United States and other members of the worldwide coalition. However, Eritrea also supports Islamist insurgents operating in Somalia. After Ethiopia invaded Somalia with U.S. backing to seize power from the Islamic Courts Union, a Taliban-style grouping of Islamist militias, a war resulted. Eritrea gave weapons to the Islamic Courts Union and provided safe haven for members of al Qaeda.

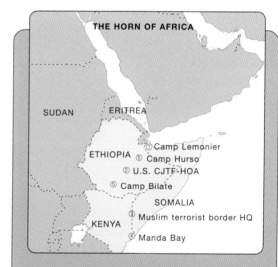

THE HORN OF AFRICA

SUDAN

ERITREA

ETHIOPIA

① Camp Lemonier

⑤ Camp Hurso

② U.S. CJTF-HOA

⑤ Camp Bilate

SOMALIA

③ Muslim terrorist border HQ

KENYA

④ Manda Bay

EIJM

The Eritrean Islamic Jihad Movement (EIJM) is composed of Islamist terrorists financed by the Islamic government in Sudan. The EIJM seeks to depose the current government in Eritrea and replace it with an Islamic theocracy based upon Sharia Law. Led by Sheikh Khalil Muhammad Amer, the EIJM claims to represent the aspirations of Eritrea's Muslim population (50 percent and growing). They are, however, based in Khartoum, Sudan, and they launch most of their terrorist raids from Sudanese soil.

The People's Front for Democracy and Justice (PFDJ), the ruling party in Eritrea, confirmed close ties between the EIJM and the Sudanese government by showing how Sudan provided the EIJM with weapons and a safe haven. The EIJM includes members of the Munezemet Arrewad al Muslimin al Eritrea (Eritrean Pioneer Muslim Organization), the Jebhat Tahrir al Eritrea al Islamiya Wataniya (Eritrean National Islamic Liberation Front), the Lejnet al Difae al Islami (Islamic Defense Committee), the Harekat al Mustedafeen al Eritrea (Movement of Oppressed Eritreans), and al Intifada Islamiya (Islamic Uprising).

A Kenyan Muslim prays during morning Eid prayers at the Sir Ali Muslim club in Nairobi, Kenya, in November 2006.

Kenya is an important partner in the U.S. Combined Joint Task Force–Horn of Africa (CJTF-HOA) in Djibouti that seeks to check terrorism. The program envisages the U.S. training of regional militaries in counter-terrorism procedures. As part of the multinational campaign, a special antiterrorism squad, composed of the German Naval Air Wing, was based in Mombasa to monitor shipping sailing in the Gulf of Aden and the Somali coast.

The White House saw Kenya as a frontline state in the war on terrorism and as a vital bulwark against its volatile neighbor, Somalia, and its many Jihadists. Terrorists have occasionally slipped across Kenya's border, as in 1998, when al Qaeda bombed the U.S. embassies in Kenya and Tanzania, another neighbor of Somalia. In 2007, the Bush administration granted the government of Kenyan president Mwai Kibaki about $1 billion in military and other aid.

U.S. FORCES IN KENYA

U.S. forces in Kenya are commanded by the Combined Joint Task Force-Horn of Africa (CJTF-HOA) and are deployed from Camp Lemonier in Djibouti. The vision of CJTF-HOA is to build friendships, forge relationships, and create partnerships, while integrating diplomacy, development, and defense efforts essential to ensuring success. With effective partnerships, the hope is that partner nations will see increased security, improved stability, and strengthened sovereignty.

At the Kenyan naval base at Manda Bay, U.S. sailors and anti-terrorism instructors from the U.S. State Department work with Kenyan law enforcement students, providing training for small-boat operations. The course is designed to train Kenyan military members in the skills and techniques used by the U.S. Navy.

Somalia, a country on the northeast coast of Africa, is one of the world's poorest. For the past decade, it has had no central government and warring clans keep the country in a state of constant civil war. Its Transitional National Government (TNG), set up in 2000, does not even control all of the capital, Mogadishu. With a 99 percent Muslim population, Somalia has seen increased radical activity in recent years. In 1993, Osama bin Laden issued a fatwa (religious decree) exhorting Somalis to drive U.S. forces out of Somalia. He also sent aides to Somalia to assist Mohamed Farah Aideed, a warlord who was resisting UN efforts to restore order during a time of civil war and famine. After UN troops were withdrawn in 1994, U.S. officials say al Qaeda continued to use Somalia as a base.

An oil tanker off the coast of Somalia. In recent years pirates have been attacking international shipping from bases in Somalia—a sign of the country's lawlessness.

ETHIOPIAN TERRORISTS

Despite Ethiopian efforts to appear as the global coalition's staunchest ally in the war on terrorism, reports are surfacing that the Ethiopian regime has actively supported Harakat al Khalas al Islami (Eritrean Islamic Salvation Movement), a movement known to have strong links to al Qaeda. The U.S. Department of State has listed the group as an al Qaeda affiliate.

A decision to actively support the Eritrean Islamist group was made by the Ethiopian regime in mid-1998, following the outbreak of the war between Ethiopia and Eritrea. In August 1999, Ethiopia's former intelligence and security chief Kinfe Gebre-Medhin met with senior members of Harkat Al Khalas Al Islami in Mekkele, the capital of Tigray Province. Ethiopia then transferred a consignment of weapons to that group, as well as to another group known as the Eritrean Islamic Jihaad. As far as is currently known, senior Ethiopian military officers are still involved in providing military support to both of these groups and apparently consider that this support best serves the foreign policy interests of Ethiopia.

SUDAN

The Sudanese government was a strong partner in the War on Terror and aggressively pursued terrorist operations directly involving threats to U.S. interests and personnel in Sudan. In 2006, Osama bin Laden and other al Qaeda leaders called for an expansion of al Qaeda's presence in Sudan in response to a possible deployment of UN peacekeepers in Darfur. Bin Laden's statement of April 23, for example, was strongly critical of the peace agreement that had been signed between Sudan's military-Islamist central government and the Sudan People's Liberation Movement (SPLM) in January 2005. Disregarding the non-Muslim identity of the southern Sudanese, bin Laden stated: "Nobody, whoever he is, has the right to accede an inch of the land of Islam, and the south will remain an inseparable part of the land of Islam."

By 2008, Sudan was being ranked by Western intelligence agencies as the third most unstable nation in the world. The United States was still cooperating with the government of Sudan on counter-terrorism, but concerns remained, particularly about the presence of certain groups within Sudan, including Hamas and Palestinian Islamic Jihad. Sudan remained on the list of State Sponsors of Terrorism.

SANCTIONS ON SUDAN

On May 29, 2007, responding to Sudanese President Bashir's continued refusal to honor his commitments to end the violence in Darfur, Sudan, U.S. president George W. Bush ordered the U.S. Treasury Department to block the assets of three Sudanese individuals and one company involved in the violence and to sanction 30 companies owned or controlled by the government of Sudan.

These designations sought to increase the political pressure on Khartoum to end the violence and supplement sanctions that the United States has maintained on Sudan since 1997. Those sanctions include restrictions on imports from and exports to Sudan, restrictions on financial transactions, an asset freeze against the government of Sudan, and a prohibition on U.S. arms sales or transfers to Sudan. Additionally, with United States leadership, the United Nations Security Council adopted Resolution 1672 (2006), which requires states to apply targeted sanctions in the form of a travel ban and an asset freeze on four specific individuals held responsible for impeding the peace process and committing heinous crimes against the people of Darfur. In Resolutions 1556 (2004) and 1591 (2005), the Security Council also imposed a partial arms embargo prohibiting arms transfers to the government of Sudan in Darfur and to all non-governmental persons operating in Darfur.

A U.S. C-130 Hercules transport aircraft takes off from a Sudanese airfield. Despite recent cooperation with the United States, Sudan has historic links with al-Qaeda. When al-Qaeda leader Osama bin Laden left Saudi Arabia in 1991, for example, he moved to Khartoum, where he was protected by a Sudanese regime that had recently imposed Islamic law in Sudan's northern states.

In 2007 only four Islamist terrorist attacks were recorded in Europe: Two failed bombings in Britain (the London and Glasgow attacks), and foiled plots in Germany (the Sauerland cell) and Denmark (the Glasvej case). The low number of arrests might be taken as indicating a general decrease in Jihadi activities after previous years. Indeed, European Union (EU) police forces arrested 201 suspects, 56 fewer than in 2006. However, these figures did not include arrests in Britain, which refuses to give precise statistics. Including the British data could actually result in an increase in arrests in 2006–2007.

Despite a low number of attacks, Islamist terrorism was still seen as the main threat to European security. Several European countries remained at a very high level of terrorism alert. This was the case, for instance, in France, Britain, Spain, and Belgium. On April 22, 2008, Gerard Bouman, head of the *Algemene Inlichtingen-en Veilgheidsdienst* (AIVD—Dutch domestic intelligence), said that the threat of Jihadi terrorism was rising in the Netherlands, especially since the release of the Islamophobic movie *Fitna*, made by the Dutch filmmaker and extreme-rightwing politician Geert Wilders.

A Europol (European Police) report of 2008 underscored several trends in Islamist terrorism in Europe:

• First, "although the majority of all arrested suspects for Islamist terrorism continue to be North African citizens, the member states reported a high number of arrested suspects with the nationality of the country of arrest." This seemed to confirm a rising threat of home-grown terrorism that had been seen for several years.

• Second, this increase in home-grown terrorism was partly the result of an increase in quantity and a "new quality" in Jihadi propaganda in Europe. It is widely recognized that propaganda on the Internet has a key importance in recruitment. Hence, recent developments appeared worrisome. For instance, al Qaeda's media arm, al-Sahab, offered English subtitles and

A U.S. soldier distributes a NATO leaflet in the town of Odzak in Bosnia and Herzogovina, in a bid to counter terrorism.

translations. In order to target specific audiences, certain Jihadi websites decided to translate Jihadi material into other languages, such as German, despite apparent difficulties in using the language correctly.

Recruitment constitutes an important part of Jihadi activities in Europe, and arrests related to it have increased. The observed developments in propaganda and recruitment suggest that al Qaeda is taking root in Europe and could potentially become stronger in the near future. On April 18, 2008, European ministers of justice reached an agreement to outlaw, among other things, online propaganda and recruitment. The new law—if approved by the European Parliament—would facilitate EU cooperation with Internet providers and, eventually, allow identification of cyber-terrorists. According to Gilles de Kerchove d'Ousselghem, EU counterterrorism coordinator, there were approximately 5,000 Jihadi Websites in existence that contributed to the radicalization of European youth.

• Third, propaganda and recruitment serve multiple purposes. Some would-be Jihadis are recruited to carry out operations in their own countries. Some are "self-recruited" through the media, and constitute a "new generation" of terrorists. Some limit their support to financing terrorism. Others decide to join the Jihad abroad: in Iraq, which remained the main destination for European fighters; in Afghanistan; or, increasingly (according to French intelligence), in Somalia.

• Finally, an interesting trend relative to Islamist terrorism in Europe concerns judicial sentences. In 2007, one-third of Jihadi terrorist suspects were acquitted, while only one-fifth of separatist terrorists were discharged. This seemed to indicate two things. First, the emphasis on Islamist terrorism by security services led to a certain "paranoia" and abusive arrests that could ultimately hurt European efforts in countering radicalization. Second, the better record in jailing separatist terrorists proved that European intelligence agencies had a greater knowledge of separatist groups and more effective strategies to counter them than was the case with Islamist terrorism.

European Muslims became increasingly susceptible to radicalization on the basis of social and political marginalization (alienation) in their host countries after 2001. Conservative Muslims' outcry over France's 2004 ban on conspicuous religious symbols (including Muslim headscarves) in schools as anti-Islamic—as well as al Qaeda second-in-command Ayman al-Zawahiri's claim that it reflected "Crusader envy"—is only the most obvious example of this "universalization" of grievances among European Muslims (who number around 30 million in total). Yet the fact that three of the five chief suspects in the Madrid bombings (see page 26) were Moroccans—many of whom were hostile to Spain over its colonial history in Morocco—also suggests that terrorists continue to be inspired by traditional concerns relating to their homelands. With two potential sources of aggrievement, European Muslims appear especially susceptible to Osama bin Laden's pan-Islamic agenda.

Who are the terrorists?

There were around 373 Islamic terrorists operating in Western Europe between 1993 and 2004. There were more Britons than Yemenis, Sudanese, Emiratis, Lebanese, or Libyans. There were twice as many French-born terrorists as Saudis. Fully a quarter of the total were Western European nationals, many of them second- or third-generation children of immigrants or native converts to Islam. These European recruits offered a ready-made strikeforce in countries previously singled out by al Qaeda's strategic planners.

AQIM

The Algerian terrorist group al Qaeda in the Islamic Maghreb (AQIM) poses a serious threat to Western Europe. The emergence of a new al Qaeda-linked organization in Northern Africa is particularly alarming to Spain, which is concerned about Islamists' calls for the reconquest of the country they regard as a lost part of the Muslim world. "We will not be in peace until we set our foot again in our beloved al-Andalus," an al Qaeda leader in the Islamic Maghreb said on claiming responsibility for an attack that killed at least 24 people in Algiers. Andalus is the Moorish name for Spain, parts of which were ruled by Muslims for about eight centuries until the last Moorish bastion, Granada, succumbed to the Christian Reconquest in 1492. The Americans have set up the Trans-Sahara Counterterrorism Initiative (TSCTI) to assist governments in North Africa to better control their territory and to prevent huge tracts of largely deserted African territory from becoming a safe haven for terrorist groups.

NATO aimed to bring stability to the Balkans by leading a peacekeeping mission in Kosovo and assisting the governments of Bosnia and Herzegovina and the former Yugoslav Republic of Macedonia to reform their armed forces. The aim is to consolidate stability in southeast Europe and facilitate the integration of Albania, Bosnia and Herzegovina, Croatia, Montenegro, Serbia, and the former Yugoslav Republic of Macedonia into Euro-Atlantic structures. Between 1996 and 2004, NATO led an international stabilisation force in Bosnia and Herzegovina, helping the country's reconstruction after the 1992–1995 war. In addition, NATO has been leading a peacekeeping operation in Kosovo since June 1999. The Kosovo Force, or KFOR, was deployed to halt and reverse the humanitarian catastrophe that was then unfolding. Following Kosovo's declaration of independence on February 17, 2008, the Nato Alliance reaffirmed that KFOR should remain in Kosovo on the basis of UN Security Resolution

1244, as agreed by foreign ministers in December 2007, unless the Security Council decides otherwise. The NATO-led force will continue to cooperate closely with the population of Kosovo, the United Nations, the European Union, and other international bodies wherever appropriate to further develop a stable, democratic, multiethnic, and peaceful Kosovo.

U.S. and Romanian military engineers cooperate on a bridge-building project as part of NATO operations in Bosnia in 1998.

Experts say there are strong ties between al Qaeda and Chechen groups. A Chechen warlord known as Khattab is said to have met Osama bin Laden while both were fighting against the 1979–1989 Soviet occupation of Afghanistan. In addition, Zacarias Moussaoui, whom U.S. authorities have charged as the "20th hijacker" in the September 11, 2001, attacks on the United States, was reported by the *Wall Street Journal* to have been "a recruiter for al-Qaeda-backed rebels in Chechnya." Chechen militants reportedly fought alongside al Qaeda and Taliban forces against the U.S.-backed Northern Alliance in late 2001. The Taliban regime in Afghanistan was one of the few governments to recognize Chechen independence.

Deadly bombings that left 191 people dead and 1,824 injured in Madrid, Spain, were one of the worst worldwide terror attacks since the September 11, 2001, strikes on New York and Washington. In addition to the widespread carnage, the March 11, 2004, blasts targeting the Spanish capital's train network caused major psychological and political fall-out.

The country swiftly re-evaluated its contribution to U.S.-led global antiterror operations. Three days after the attacks, which were blamed on Islamic militant groups including al Qaeda, the government was voted out of office. Its successors ended Spain's military involvement in Iraq. Meanwhile, Spain launched a massive manhunt for the perpetrators, eventually bringing 29 suspects to trial in February 2007.

Red Cross workers carry bomb victims from a train outside Madrid, Spain, after the terrorist attacks of March 11, 2004.

THE AL QAEDA CONNECTION

The Madrid bombings were carried out by a group of North African Islamists that had joined forces with a band of petty criminals whose ringleader, Jamal Ahmidan, had become radicalized while incarcerated in a Moroccan jail. Seven of the main suspects, including Ahmidan, blew themselves up in a Madrid apartment when they were surrounded by the police three weeks after the attacks, and four others from the group are believed to have fled. In October 2007, some of the others who had carried out the attacks were sentenced by a Spanish court. Jamal Zougam, 34, a Moroccan, was sentenced to more than 30,000 years in prison for charges that included murder. Similar sentences were given to Otman el-Gnaoui, 32, a Moroccan national who helped to transport the explosives used in the attacks, and to José Emilio Suárez Trashorras, 30, who was convicted as a "necessary accomplice." Some suspects had been killed in the blast. These were: Sarhane ben Abdelmajid Fakhet ("El Tunecino", the Tunisian), who was the suspected ringleader of the plot; Allekema Lamari, Algerian; Mohammed Oulad Akcha and Rachid Oulad Akcha, Moroccan brothers; and Abdennabi Kounjaa (known as "Abdallah"), Moroccan.

During the morning rush hour on July 7, 2005, four explosions ripped through the London transport system, affecting three separate areas of the Underground metro system and one double-decker bus. The bombings killed 56 people, including the four Muslim bombers (Mohammad Sidique Khan, 30, Germaine Lindsay, 19, Hasib Hussain, 18, and Shehzad Tanweer, 22), and injured more than 700. Two weeks later, on July 21, four unexploded devices were also found in London—three on subway trains and one on a bus. On July 9, 2007, three men—Muktar Said Ibrahim, 29, Yassin Omar, 26, and Ramzi Mohammed, 25—were found guilty of conspiracy to murder and were sent to jail for a minimum of 40 years. The attacks led to changes in laws on the advocacy of terrorism and a crackdown on the radical fundamentalist Islamic community.

The wreckage of a London double-decker bus blown apart by a terrorist bomb in the British capital city on July 7, 2005.

The European Police Office (known as "Europol") is an international police organization that was formed to promote cooperation among law enforcement agencies within the European Union. The establishment of the Europol agency was first agreed upon on February 7, 1992, in the Treaty on European Union, and Europol began its full range of activities on July 1, 1999. Its main aim is to ensure the sharing of information and the coordination of operations among the police forces of all 25 European Union (EU) member states.

In order to fight international organized crime effectively, Europol also cooperates with a number of third parties: Albania, Australia, Bosnia and Herzegovina, Canada, Colombia, Croatia, former Yugoslav Republic of Macedonia, Iceland, Interpol, Moldova, Norway, Russian Federation, Switzerland, and Turkey.

A true Europe-wide agency?

In 2007, there were 48 percent more terrorism arrests—a total of 1,044—than in 2006. The "Europe-wide" terror threat, however, seems (if it is measured by police activity) to be largely illusory, because there are really only three countries actively involved: France, Spain, and Britain led the rest of Europe in terms of arrest numbers, with 409, 261, and 203 respectively. However, most of these arrests were not related to Islamic terrorism. Many of the French and Spanish arrests, for example, were related to crackdowns on Basque and Corsican separatist groups.

MUSLIMS IN BRITAIN

There are 1.6 million Muslims among the total British population of approximately 60 million people. Nearly 60 percent of the Muslim population hold British citizenship and many of them were born in Britain. Muslim immigrants tend to hail from former colonial territories such as Pakistan, India, and Bangladesh. The Muslim Council of Britain serves as the community's lobby group, and Muslims tend to be more active in politics than other minorities.

Muslims in Britain reportedly face a considerable amount of discrimination, especially in the aftermath of September 11, 2001. They have the lowest employment rate among members of all religions and tend to live in segregated communities. In the year following 9/11, the Islamic Human Rights Commission reported 344 violent incidents against Muslims; another spike occurred after the March 11, 2004, Madrid train bombings. Muslims also face targeting from law enforcement. They are part of the most likely demographic to be stopped and searched, and the ratio of terror-related arrests to convictions is disproportionately high.

COUNTERTERRORIST AGENCIES

These are the intelligence agencies leading the war on terror in Europe:

Britain
MI5—Security Service. Responsible for the internal security of the United Kingdom.
MI6—Secret Intelligence Service. Gathers information and recruits agents abroad.

France
DST—Directorate of Territorial Surveillance. An internal security agency whose function is to search for information for security and to monitor terrorist threats.

Germany
DGSE—General Directorate for External Security. Responsible for military intelligence, as well as for strategic information, electronic intelligence, and counterespionage.

In the 1990s, Pakistan provided the Taliban with advisers and war materials in its battles with rival warlords, ensuring Pakistan a friendly government that controlled most of Afghanistan. However, the Taliban also hosted unsavory guests, including al Qaeda, which by the late 1990s had been identified as a serious new threat by the United States. Following the 9/11 attacks and the U.S.-led invasion of Afghanistan that followed, leaders of al Qaeda and the Afghan Taliban, along with several other terrorist groups, fled across the border into Pakistan and made its Federally Administered Tribal Areas (FATA) their new home.

Terrorist groups in Pakistan

Many terrorist groups operate in Pakistan. These include the Afghan Taliban, consisting of the original Taliban movement and its Kandahari leadership centered around Mullah Mohammad Omar, who is believed to be now living in Quetta. Also in Pakistan is al Qaeda and its affiliates. The organization led by Osama bin Laden and other non-South Asian terrorists are believed to be ensconced in the Federally Administered Tribal Areas (FATA). Other foreign militant groups, such as the Islamic Movement of Uzbekistan, Islamic Jihad Group, the Libyan Islamic Fighters Group, and the Eastern Turkistan Islamic Movement are also located in FATA. In addition, also in the region are the Pakistani "Taliban," groups consisting of extremist outfits led by individuals such as Baitullah Mehsud, the chieftain of the Mehsud tribe in South Waziristan; Maulana Faqir Muhammad and Maulana Qazi Fazlullah of the Tehrik-e-Nafaz-e-Shariat-e-Mohammadi (TSNM); and Mangal Bagh Afridi of the Lashkar-e-Islami in the Khyber Agency.

In November 2008, terrorist attacks in India's financial capital, Mumbai (which the Indian government blamed on Pakistan-based militants), increased tension between India and Pakistan. Yet cooperation between the two would seem essential to the War on Terror. In September 2008, therefore, the Bush administration formed a "Friends for Pakistan"

group to work with Pakistan on issues such as stability, development, and institution building. The group includes China and Saudi Arabia, which hold considerable influence over Pakistan's military and political elite.

The ISI problem

Pakistan's stability also has ramifications for Washington's broader regional interests. Roughly 80 percent of all U.S. and NATO supplies headed for the Afghan theater transit through Pakistan, but unrest and road closures have prompted the Pentagon to explore alternative supply lines passing through Central Asia. The Mumbai attacks also renewed suspicions that all parts of the Pakistani governmental apparatus, and particularly its strong military and notorious intelligence agency, the Inter-Services Intelligence (ISI), might not wholly support Washington's fight against terrorism. Some analysts believe the army and the ISI are reluctant to sever ties with militant groups they have long used to pursue Pakistani national interests in Afghanistan and Indian-administered Kashmir. This has led to calls for Washington to break from its narrow focus on military and intelligence cooperation with Islamabad. The United States has long pursued short-term stability in Pakistan by sending aid to Pakistan's military and individual leaders. Pakistan currently ranks among the largest recipients of U.S. military aid; the Pakistani military relies on the United States for roughly a quarter of its $4 billion budget.

Washington's Number 1 problem

Pakistan is a top concern for the new Obama administration. In particular, its lawless northwest tribal region, which acts as a terrorist sanctuary for militants from around the world, has become central to winning the U.S.-led war in Afghanistan, ensuring a stable South Asia, and curbing global terrorism. The problem is made worse by the always fractious relationship between Indian and Pakistan, two nuclear-armed states who have gone to war on three occasions since 1947 and distrust each other intently. This is not good news for Washington's War on Terror.

Eyes in the sky—a U.S. Predator unmanned drone is prepared for a reconnaissance mission over the Afghan–Pakistan border region.

THE PAKISTAN–AFGHAN BORDER

The Pakistan-Afghan border region is 1,000 miles (1,620 km) long and 100 miles (162 km) wide. It is a haven for bandits, religious and tribal violence, heroin laboratories, and weapons smugglers. Both NATO and the Afghan government claim that the Taliban have created a sanctuary in this belt along Pakistan's frontier, giving support to the insurgency in Afghanistan.

In 2006, the Pakistanis decided to establish a security zone about 1.5 miles (3 km) wide in North Waziristan. They were eager to show they were on top of border security, because they had been criticized for ceding control to pro-Taliban tribesmen. For more than a year, the Pakistani Army waged a military campaign against foreign militants in this area, but the tactic backfired. It led to fierce fighting, and radicalized the local tribesmen, turning them toward the Taliban.

So the Pakistan government signed a peace deal, aimed at returning power to the tribal elders who had lost influence to the pro-Taliban militants. The Pakistan government also signed a peace deal with the tribes in neighboring South Waziristan.

In March 2008, Afghan, NATO, and Pakistani officials opened the first of six intelligence-sharing centers to be established along the troubled border region in order to boost antiterrorism efforts. The centers opened in the key Afghan border town of Torkham, along with the others, will improve coordination between Afghanistan, Pakistan, and NATO's International Security Assistance Force (ISAF) in the fight against extremists.

A Pakistan military official escorts a captured militant in Wana, Pakistan, in March 2004. Nearly 100 suspects were taken into custody after fighting in Pakistan's South Waziristan.

VIOLENCE IN KASHMIR

The region of Kashmir, situated in northern India, is in the grip of violence between the Hindu and Muslim populations. The conflict was triggered by the Indian government's decision to transfer land in the Muslim-majority state to establish a Hindu shrine. The ensuing violence was the culmination of a rise in communal tensions between Hindus and Muslims.

NATO fears that such deteriorating conditions in Kashmir could encourage Pakistan-based militants who have been gaining strength in the tribal areas of the country. Political turmoil in Pakistan has also worsened prospects of sustained peace with India.

The Pakistani Army and its intelligence services have been accused of backing separatist militants in Kashmir. The crisis in Kashmir also poses problems for U.S. counterterrorism efforts in the region. If Kashmir sparks a new India–Pakistan crisis, it could put at risk critical U.S. interests.

The position of Pakistan

The accusation has some merit. Pakistan has long nurtured the militant group Lashkar-e-Taiba (LeT) as a way of pursuing a Kashmir setttlement. At the end of 2008 President Zardari and army chief Ashfaq Pervez Kiyani showed signs that Pakistan was going to crack down on LeT, cut ties with terrorists, and stand firmly against extremism. However, this approach posed risks, not least because there are thousands of LeT operatives in Pakistan who have benefited from years of training in the tactics of insurgency. The group would be likely to react to any crackdown with a spate of suicide bombings, assassinations, and kidnappings.

KASHMIR

The territory of Kashmir, currently divided between India and Pakistan by the Line of Control (LOC), has been hotly contested ever since the two countries were partitioned in August 1947 (China also controls a small portion of Kashmir). Indian-administered Kashmir has been a hotbed of insurgency since 1989, and the LOC itself is disputed; India wants it to be recognized as an international border, but Pakistan refuses. However, a peace process in 2004 approached the issue from a different angle by advancing the idea of making borders irrelevant through increasing trade, and facilitating greater people-to-people contact across the LOC. However, the tensions that erupted in 2008 shattered this proposal.

AL QAEDA IN PAKISTAN

In September 2008, Admiral Mike Mullen, chairman of the U.S. Joint Chiefs of Staff, held meetings with Pakistani military and security leaders to discuss allowing the Americans access to the Pakistan–Afghan border region, where al Qaeda terrorists have been regrouping and setting up training and operations bases. U.S. drones (unmanned aircraft) operate over the border, and have struck several times in northwest Pakistan in 2008, killing dozens of suspected militants. However, in June 2008 Pakistan was outraged when 11 soldiers were killed in a U.S. air strike, which had been ordered after NATO forces came under fire from militants in Pakistan's Mohmand tribal region. As a result, it seems unlikely that Pakistan will allow NATO forces into the border area to destroy al Qaeda and Taliban safe havens.

Unwelcome guests?

The Director of National Intelligence, J. Michael McConnell, told the Senate Armed Services Committee in his February 2008 annual threat assessment report that al Qaeda's "central leadership based in the border area of Pakistan is its most dangerous component." However, there are signs that the organization might be out-living its welcome in Pakistan. Many Pakistanis have turned against al-Qaeda and bin Laden. In a poll released in February 2008, Terror Free Tomorrow, a Washington-based nonprofit group, found that only 24 percent of Pakistanis had a favorable opinion of bin Laden in 2008, as compared to 46 percent in August 2007. Similarly, al-Qaeda's popularity dropped from 33 percent to 18 percent.

U.S. FINANCIAL AID

In June 2008, the U.S. government reported that nearly $11 billion in military and economic assistance grants had been delivered to its allies in the war on terror since 2002, the vast majority channeled through Pakistan's military for security-related programs. A report by the Center for Public Integrity found that in the three years after the 9/11 attacks, military aid to Pakistan from the Coalition Support Fund—created after the attacks to assist U.S. allies in the global fight against terrorism—was nearly $3 billion. Pakistan has used the money to purchase helicopters, F-16 planes, aircraft-mounted armaments, and antiship and antimissile defense systems—weapons that Indian officials and others have deemed of questionable relevance to the counterterrorism mission.

FIGHTING IN WAZIRISTAN

In the rugged and remote region of Waziristan on Pakistan's northwest border with Afghanistan, Islamic rebels allied to the Afghan Taliban and al Qaeda are battling to establish an Islamic Republic. The fighting began in 2004, when Pakistan's army entered the region in search of al Qaeda and Taliban fighters who were using Waziristan as a base for attacks against U.S. and Allied forces in Afghanistan.

Since the fighting began, Pakistani forces suffer almost daily casualties due to roadside bombs and ambushes. The authority of the central government is almost nonexistent in the rebellious tribal borderlands. The United States aids Pakistan with intelligence information and with tactical airstrikes on suspected rebel bases. The best known U.S. airstrike occurred at the village of Damadola, on January 13, 2006. This Predator-drone attack killed at least 18 people, including several non-Waziri foreign al Qaeda fighters.

In July 2007, following nearly 10 months of an uneasy peace, the Islamic militants of Waziristan once again began fighting the Pakistani government in

Pakistani troops guard an area of the Mohmand Agency on the border with Afghanistan in August 2003.

response to the siege of and army assault on the Red Mosque in Islamabad. The Red Mosque had been held by Islamic militants whom the Pakistani Army ousted in a bloody battle.

The U.S. had been critical of President Musharaff's Pakistan government for letting the militants in the Waziristan border region regroup during the 10-month truce. After the violence reignited, Washington offered assistance to Pakistan in terms of arms and other aid. Rumors of possible U.S. intervention against the Taliban and al Qaeda in Waziristan sparked a rebuke from the Pakistani government that any such cross-border action would be opposed.

THE NEW MILITANTS

Al Qaeda is now training most of the terrorist groups in Pakistan's tribal border areas. Pakistan's tribal areas are also experiencing growing extremism. Like their Taliban predecessors in Afghanistan, the younger militants consider music, TV, and luxuries like massage parlors un-Islamic and wage war against them. Local Taliban leaders in the tribal agencies tell men to keep beards and women to wear the veil.

There is growing criticism both within and outside Pakistan that the army does not have the capacity to fight insurgency within its borders. Militants increasingly target the army with suicide attacks and in August 2007, the kidnapping of around 250 soldiers by Baitullah Mehsud in FATA's South Waziristan posed a huge embarrassment for Pakistan.

THE ISI

Pakistan's intelligence agency, the Inter-Services Intelligence (ISI), has long faced accusations of meddling in the affairs of its neighbors. After 2001 a range of officials from both inside and outside of Pakistan stepped up their suggestions of links between the ISI and terrorist groups. In autumn 2006, for example, a leaked report by a British Defense Ministry think-tank reinforced this view, when it stated, "Indirectly Pakistan (through the ISI) has been supporting terrorism and extremism—whether in London on 7/7, or in Afghanistan, or Iraq." In June 2008, Afghan officials accused Pakistan's intelligence service of plotting a failed assassination attempt on Afghanistan's President Hamid Karzai; shortly thereafter, the Afghan leadership implied that the ISI was involved in the July 2008 attack on the Indian embassy.

On Pakistan's western border with Afghanistan, the ISI supported the Taliban up to September 11, 2001, and experts generally suspect that Pakistan continues to provide some support to the Taliban. However, Pakistan has arrested scores of al Qaeda operatives and affiliates, including Khalid Sheikh Mohammed, the alleged mastermind behind the 9/11 attacks on the United States in 2001. In addition, the ISI and the Pakistani military have worked effectively alongside the United States to pursue the remnants of al Qaeda within Pakistan's borders. Following 9/11, Pakistan stationed 80,000 troops in the troubled province of Waziristan near the Afghan border, where several hundred Pakistani soldiers have subsequently been killed in the resulting battles and clashes with al Qaeda militants.

BACKING BOTH SIDES

Pakistan has two policies when it comes to the war on terror. One is an official policy of promoting stability in Afghanistan; the other is an unofficial policy of supporting Jihadis in order to appease political forces within Pakistan. Pakistan does not enjoy good relations with the leadership of Afghanistan, partly because of disagreements with Afghan President Hamid Karzai, and partly because Karzai has developed strong ties with India. Consequently, Pakistan wants to see a stable, friendlier government emerge in Afghanistan. In addition, supporting the Taliban also allows Pakistan to hedge its bets should the NATO coalition pull out of Afghanistan. The Pakistani intelligence services continue to support the Taliban because they see the Taliban leadership "as a strategic asset," a reliable back-up force in case things go sour in Afghanistan.

AL QAEDA IN INDIA

Flames light up the sky in Mumbai, India, as the Taj Hotel comes under terrorist attack in November 2008.

There are currently many terrorist groups operating in India, a country that has a population of nearly a billion. India is home to 150 million Muslims, the second largest Muslim population in the world, but many of them feel they are discriminated against by their government and by the security forces. This makes them receptive to the aims of al Qaeda.

Pro-al Qaeda Jihadi organizations from Pakistan have been active in Indian territory since 1993. These groups are: Lashkar-e-Taiba (LeT), "Army of the Pure"; Jaish-e-Muhammad, meaning "Army of Mohammad," Harakat ul-Mujahedeen (HuM) or the "Islamic Freedom Fighters' Group"; and Harakat ul-Jihad-I-Islami (HUJI).

All these five militant groups share a defiant opposition to Western-style liberal democracy, and all support the creation of a global Islamic Caliphate, which, according to them, will be governed by the will of Allah, as interpreted by the clerics.

INDIA'S INTELLIGENCE AGENCIES

India has several intelligence agencies that monitor terrorist activities. The Research and Analysis Wing (RAW) is the external intelligence agency and the Intelligence Bureau (IB), a division of the Home Affairs Ministry, collects intelligence inside India. A Joint Intelligence Committee analyzes intelligence data from RAW and IB, as well as from a handful of military intelligence agencies, which usually provide tactical information gathered while carrying out counterterrorist operations.

The IB oversees an interagency counterterrorism center similar to the CIA. The Ministry of External Affairs oversees its own counterterrorism body, much like the U.S. State Department, which oversees diplomatic counterterrorism functions, such as briefing other nations on suspected Pakistani sponsorship of terrorism in India.

Operation Iraqi Freedom (OIF)—the U.S.-led coalition's military operation in Iraq—was launched on March 20, 2003. The immediate goal, as stated by the Bush administration, was to remove Saddam Hussein's regime, including destroying its ability to build or use weapons of mass destruction or to make them available to terrorists.

The broad, longer-term objectives of the campaign included helping the Iraqi people to build "a new Iraq that is prosperous and free." In October 2002, the U.S. Congress had authorized the U.S. president to use force against Iraq to "defend the national security of the United States against the continuing threat posed by Iraq" and to "enforce all relevant United Nations Security Council resolutions regarding Iraq."

Rebuilding Iraq

After the initial combat operations, the focus of OIF shifted from regime removal to the more open-ended mission of helping an emerging new Iraqi leadership to improve security, establish a system of governance, and foster economic development. Over time, serious challenges to the Iraqi leadership from home-grown insurgents and from foreign fighters mounted. Sectarian violence grew, catalyzed by the February 2006 bombing of the Golden Mosque in Samarra. Accordingly, the character of the war evolved from major combat operations to a multifaceted counter-insurgency (COIN) and reconstruction effort.

In January 2007, in an attempt to reverse the escalation of violence, President George W. Bush announced a fresh strategic approach to Iraq, called the "New Way Forward," which included a "surge" of additional U.S. forces to be deployed into the country. The troop surge included five Army brigade combat teams (BCTs), a Marine Expeditionary Unit (MEU), and two Marine battalions. More importantly, most impartial observers agree, the surge institutionalized COIN approaches on the ground, designed to promote

A cavalry scouting unit from the U.S. 1st Infantry Division leads the advance through southern Fallujah in Iraq in January 2005 as part of the U.S.-led Operation Iraqi Freedom. The city of Fallujah is located in the Iraqi province of Al Anbar, approximately 43 miles (69 km) west of Baghdad on the Euphrates River.

population security, such as troops living among the local population at small outposts.

Over the course of the surge, security conditions on the ground improved markedly. In August 2008, the outgoing Commanding General of Multi-National Force-Iraq, General David Petraeus, agreed that there had been "significant progress," but argued that it was "still not self-sustaining."

From an operational perspective, the year 2008 witnessed several major but uneven transitions. First, the substantial security improvements achieved over the course of the "surge" continued to hold and grow further, with some fluctuations during combat operations in specific regions. Second, most experts believed that the operational capabilities of the Iraqi Security Forces (ISF) continued to grow, reflected in—and encouraged by—ISF operational experiences in Basra, Sadr City, Amarah, Mosul, and Diyala. According to U.S. commanders, the March 2008 ISF operations in Basra, targeting Shi'a militias, were poorly planned and required a strong rescue effort by coalition forces. The August operations in Diyala, targeting affiliates of al Qaeda in Iraq (AQI), were planned by the Iraqis in advance, but still required coalition forces to help to hold onto areas once they were cleared of militants. Some U.S. officials suggest that the ultimate success of these operations has given Iraqi leaders disproportionate confidence in the capabilities of the ISF.

The Iraqis take the reins of power

Meanwhile, U.S. personnel in Iraq, both civilian and military, suggest that the appetite of Iraqi officials to be advised or guided by U.S. mentors is diminishing. Over time, and particularly as Iraqi capacity and capabilities grew and as Iraqi confidence in those capabilities increased, Iraqi officials have demonstrated growing assertiveness and less inclination to consult with U.S. advisers before taking action. Examples were the decision by Prime Minister Nouri al Maliki to launch military operations in Basra, and the Iraqi government's stated intent to accelerate its assumption of full responsibility for Iraq. The ability of the U.S. government to shape the course of events in Iraq seemed to be diminishing.

The main ground assault into Iraq was led by U.S. Army V Corps, which was assigned the western route up to Baghdad, west of the Euphrates River. Meanwhile, the 1st Marine Expeditionary Force (1MEF) was assigned the eastern route, closer to the border with Iran. From a tactical perspective, for both the Army and the Marines this was a very long projection of force—370 miles (600 km) from Kuwait to Baghdad, and more for those units that pushed farther north to Tikrit or to Mosul. Those distances strained logistics and communications. The U.S. Marines on the eastern route to Baghdad had more urban areas to deal with than the U.S. Army's western route, such as the southern port city of Umm Qasr. The basic strategy still called for a quick drive to Baghdad.

The British 1st Armoured Division, which fell under 1MEF, was tasked to take Basra, Iraq's second largest city. The British faced resistance from the paramilitary force Saddam Fedayeen and others still loyal to the Ba'ath Party. To limit casualties, rather than enter the city immediately in full force the division used a more methodical elimination of opponents, combined with an outreach program to the population to explain their intentions. IMEF supported the division's use of a slow and deliberate tempo. After weeks of gradual attrition, the division pushed into Basra on April 6, 2003.

INVASION OF IRAQ

Date   March 20–May 1, 2003

Commanders and forces   United Nations: 270,000 troops (General Tommy Ray Franks); Iraqi: 375,000 troops (Saddam Hussein)

Casualties   United Nations: 171 killed; Iraqi: 10,800 killed

Key actions   The main IMEF force encountered some resistance as they pushed north, in particular at the town of Nassiriyah. The U.S. Marines suffered casualties from a "friendly fire" incident with Apache helicopters. As widely reported, the Army's 507th Maintenance Company lost its way in the area and stumbled into an ambush, in which some personnel were killed and others, including PFC Jessica Lynch, were taken hostage. The 3rd Infantry Division rapidly led the western charge to Baghdad, moving speedily through the south and reaching Saddam International Airport on April 4. On April 9, the statue of Saddam Hussein in Firdos Square in Baghdad was toppled. This event signaled for many observers, inside and outside Iraq, that the old Iraqi regime had ended.

Key effects   Iraqi dictator Saddam Hussein was removed from power and a U.S.-sponsored government was installed to replace him. However, the Iraqi Army and police force were both disbanded, allowing home-grown and foreign extremists to wage war against UN forces.

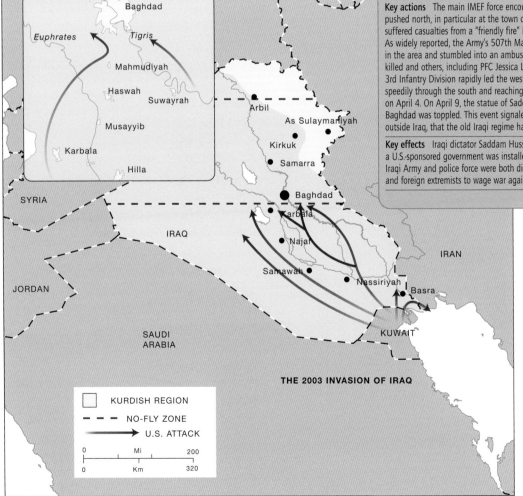

THE 2003 INVASION OF IRAQ

KURDISH REGION

– – – NO-FLY ZONE

→ U.S. ATTACK

A sniper from the U.S. 82nd Airborne Division's 1st Battalion trains his rifle on a rooftop during a search mission in Fallujah, Iraq.

The insurgency in Iraq grew from early 2004 from 25 attacks per day to 60 by the year's end. Around 80 percent of all attacks occurred in Sunni-dominated central Iraq. Sunni Arabs, dominated by Ba'athist and Former Regime Elements (FRE), comprised the core of the insurgency. Shi'as, oppressed for decades under the rule of Saddam, also attacked Coalition forces, and foreign fighters also joined the insurgency. Syrian, Saudi, Egyptian, Jordanian, and Iranian nationals made up the majority of foreign fighters. Fighters, arms, and other supplies continued to enter Iraq from virtually all of its neighbors, despite increased border security.

THE INSURGENCY SPREADS

Location   Iraq

Date   January–December 2004

Commanders and forces   Iraqi terrorists: 200,000 part-time fighters and volunteers (Abu Musab al-Zarqawi)

Casualties   Coalition: 906 killed; insurgents: 6,801 killed

Key actions   **March 2:** In the Ashoura Massacre, almost 200 are killed in a series of bomb blasts in Baghdad and Karbala; **April 16:** Kut is retaken by Coalition forces, but Najaf, Karbala, and Kufa remain under the control of al-Sadr; **June 28:** Control and sovereignty of Iraq are handed over from the United States to an interim Iraqi government; **October 1:** An early-morning, coordinated invasion of Samarra by 3,000 U.S. troops and 2,000 Iraqi troops begins.

Key effects   The insurgency and media revelations of prisoner abuse at Abu Ghraib prison by Coalition soldiers damaged the moral justifications for the occupation of Iraq in the eyes of many Iraqis.

Radical Shi'a leader Muqtada al-Sadr led an uprising from April to June of 2004. It took place to prevent American forces from capturing al-Sadr. The Jaish al-Mahdi (JAM) was a loose confederation of religious militias and criminal gangs raised from among the people of Baghdad (Sadr City), Basra, and a number of other large Iraqi cities.

U.S. forces quickly laid siege to JAM positions and U.S. troops killed several hundred JAM militia between April to June in Sadr City. JAM forces deserted at high rates and could not sustain military operations. The Americans divided JAM into isolated groups to prevent any central coordination.

Iraqi Shi'a militiamen keep watch for U.S. Marines and Iraqi security forces in the city of Najaf in August 2004.

THE SHI'A UPRISING

Location   Sadr City, Baghdad, Iraq

Date   April 4–June, 2004

Commanders and forces   U.S.: 1st Brigade, 1st Cavalry Division (Colonel Robert Abrams); Shi'a: 5,000 fighters (Muqtada al-Sadr)

Casualties   U.S.: 8 killed, 51 wounded; Shi'a: 800 killed

Key actions   JAM forces deserted at high rates and could not sustain military operations. American firepower was overwhelming.

Key effects   Since 2004, JAM has not launched a coordinated attack against American or Iraqi government forces. JAM splinter cells and criminal elements fought Coalition forces on isolated occasions.

BATTLE FOR FALLUJAH

The assault on Fallujah was an attempt to regain control of the city from insurgents, in preparation for national elections scheduled for January 2005. Fallujah had a population of approximately 300,000 civilians, but U.S. military officials believed that 70–90 percent of the city's population had fled. Prior to the commencement of the operation, Prime Minister Ayad Allawi declared a state of emergency across Iraq, except for the Kurdish area of the country, as violence flared in anticipation of the assault on Fallujah.

Under the cover of darkness in the early hours of November 8, 2004, six battalions of Army–Marine–Iraqi forces began the assault. An intense bombing of enemy positions was followed by a ground attack on the main railroad station, which was captured and used as a staging post for follow-on forces. By November 16, 2004, the major fighting was over and the U.S.-led force had been successful in suppressing all resistance.

BATTLE FOR FALLUJAH

Location   Fallujah, Iraq

Date   November 7–December 23, 2004

Commanders and forces   Coalition: U.S. 1st Marine Regiment, 7th Marine Regiment, 1st Cavalry Division, 1st Infantry Division, 36th Infantry Division (Texas Army National Guard); Iraqi: 4 battalions, Iraqi Intervention Force, 36th Commando Battalion, Counterterrorism Force, 1st Specialized Special Forces Battalion (General Richard F. Natonski); Insurgents: 5,000 (al Qaeda in Iraq and Mujahideen Shura of al-Falluja)

Casualties   Coalition: 106 killed, 600 wounded; Insurgents: 1,350 killed, 1,500 taken prisoner

Key actions   Shortly after nightfall on November 9, 2004, U.S. Marines were reportedly moving along Highway 10 in the center of Fallujah.

Key effects   The recapture of Fallujah proved to be a success for U.S. forces, with a large number of local insurgent fighters being killed, while the momentum the Sunni rebellion had gained from controlling the city was dashed in the face of overwhelming U.S. firepower. Further, al Qaeda's foothold in Iraq had been seriously degraded, even though its leader, Abu Musab Al-Zarqawi, managed to escape.

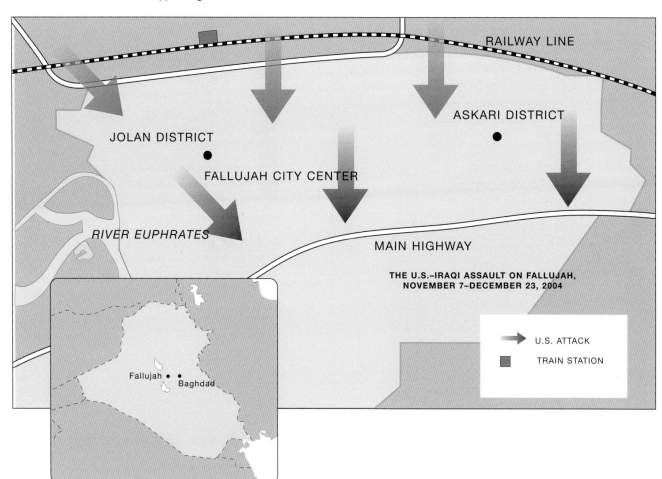

RAILWAY LINE

ASKARI DISTRICT

JOLAN DISTRICT

FALLUJAH CITY CENTER

RIVER EUPHRATES

MAIN HIGHWAY

THE U.S.–IRAQI ASSAULT ON FALLUJAH, NOVEMBER 7–DECEMBER 23, 2004

Fallujah • • Baghdad

→ U.S. ATTACK

◼ TRAIN STATION

The death tolls in Iraq, both military and civilian, since the fall of Saddam in 2003 far outstripped those during the initial period of the U.S.-led military action. Insurgent attacks became part of daily life in some areas. Two major peaks in violence came ahead of national elections in January 2005 and in the run-up to the referendum on the constitution in October 2005.

Although 80 percent of insurgent attacks were targeted against Coalition forces, the Iraqi population suffered about 80 percent of all casualties. From late 2004, the number of attacks on Iraqi security personnel increased, as the newly-constituted army and police force grew and became active. The figures also showed a significant increase in attacks on civilians in the months following the bombing of a key Shi'a mosque in Samarra in February 2006, which unleashed new levels of sectarian violence between Sunnis and Shi'as.

Insurgent attacks also became more sophisticated. The numbers of explosions from car bombs, suicide car bombs, and roadside bombs all doubled from 2004 to 2005. The number of multiple-fatality bombings increased from less than 20 a month in 2004 to a peak of 57 in June 2006. And from early 2005, gruesome finds of groups of corpses, often showing signs of execution or torture, became increasingly common.

By May 2006, attacks against Coalition and Iraqi units were common, especially in the "Sunni Triangle" and parts of northern Iraq. The bombing of a Shi'a mosque in Samarra in February 2006 had triggered fierce sectarian violence, resulting in a rapid increase in Iraqi civilian victims, particularly in Baghdad. Islamic radicals sought to create political chaos, giving rise to a "chain of retaliation." U.S. President Bush, after discussions with the Iraqi government, announced a new strategy in January 2007. An extra 20,000 troops were to be sent to Iraq and another carrier strike group was deployed to the Middle East. Thus was the groundwork laid for the U.S. troop surge in 2007.

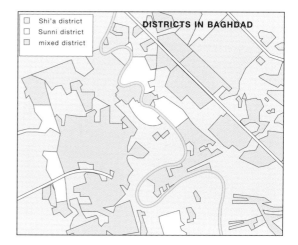

The sectarian divide in Baghdad, which erupted into violence in 2006, resulting in thousands of civilians casualties.

2005—THE VIOLENCE ESCALATES

Major attacks by insurgents in Iraq:

18 Nov 2005—80 dead Multiple bombings in Baghdad and two Khanaqin mosques

14 Sept 2005—182 dead Suicide car bomber targets Baghdad laborers

16 Aug 2005—90 dead Suicide bomber detonates fuel tanker in Musayyib

28 Feb 2005—114 dead Suicide car bomb hits government jobseekers in Hilla

24 June 2004—100 dead Coordinated blasts in Mosul and other cities

2 March 2004—140 dead Suicide bombers attack Shi'a festivals at Karbala and Baghdad

1 Feb 2004—105 dead Twin attacks on Kurdish parties' offices in Irbil

28 Aug 2003—85 dead Bomb at Najaf shrine targets senior Shi'a cleric

Large-scale killings:

7 Oct 2005—22 bodies found handcuffed and shot near the town of Badra

25 Aug 2005—36 bodies found blindfolded, handcuffed, and executed near Badra

U.S. CASUALTIES IN IRAQ IN 2006

Month	Killed	Wounded
January	61	521
February	53	300
March	30	475
April	74	481
May	69	422
June	59	512
July	42	574
August	65	503
September	70	776
October	100	870
November	63	502
December	105	644

ASSAULT ON SAMARRA

U.S. TROOP SURGE, 2007

Iraqi security forces and their Coalition partners launched "Operation Swarmer" in Salah Ad Din Province to clear suspected insurgents near Samarra. Aircraft provided aerial weapons support and delivered troops from the Iraqi Army's 4th Division, the Rakkasans from 1st and 3rd Battalions, 187th Infantry Regiment, and the Hunters from the 2d Squadron, 9th Cavalry Regiment, to multiple objectives. Forces of the 2d Commando Brigade then completed a ground infiltration to secure buildings in the area. Facing light resistance in the early stages of the operation, no airborne weapons were fired. Forces were landed by aircraft near the objective areas and quickly secured their targets.

A U.S. soldier of the 2d Battalion, 9th Cavalry Regiment, launches an unmanned spy vehicle during "Operation Swarmer" in Iraq.

ASSAULT ON SAMARRA

Location Samarra, north-central Iraq

Date March 16-22, 2006

Commanders and forces Coalition: U.S.: 101st Airborne Division's 3rd Brigade Combat Team, 101st Combat Aviation Brigade; Iraqi: 1st Brigade, 4th Division; Insurgents: al Qaeda in Iraq

Casualties Coalition: none; Insurgents: 48 taken prisoner

Key actions "Operation Swarmer" was designed to sweep 96 square miles (250 square km) of sparsely-populated desert for insurgents and their weapons. The large desert region required a substantial airborne assault on key targets.

Key effects The operation resulted in 104 suspected insurgents being detained and questioned, and 24 weapons caches being discovered. The caches included: 6 shoulder-fired surface-to-air missiles; more than 350 mortar rounds and three mortar systems; 26 artillery rounds; a variety of bomb-making materials; more than 120 rockets; more than 3,200 rounds of small-arms ammunition; 86 rocket-propelled grenades and 28 grenade launchers; 6 landmines; 12 hand grenades and 40 rifle grenades; and 34 rifles and machine guns of various types.

The Iraq Troop Surge was announced by U.S. President George W. Bush on January 10, 2007, as a new strategy for securing some bandit regions of the country by increasing the number of U.S. troops that would be operating there. The troop surge was concentrated in Baghdad and the western province of Anbar, which were the most violent parts of the country. By June 15, 2007, the surge was completed with an additional 160,000 U.S. troops.

The surge involved "embedding" U.S. forces within Iraqi units in order to assist them in suppressing insurgent activity in the two regions. This military effort was supported by other measures aimed at addressing reconstruction within the nation of Iraq and also at encouraging political progress between rival groups. At its core, the surge was about cooperatively protecting the Iraqi civilian population.

By the end of 2008, the strategy, carried out under the command of General David Petraeus, had been a remarkable success, reducing the rate of violence in Iraq by more than 80 percent, while also helping to spark the beginnings of a gradual process of political reconciliation. However, it took far more than the simple addition of 30,000 U.S. troops, on top of the 140,000 already there when the surge began, to make this happen.

SUCCESS OF THE U.S. TROOP SURGE

The following factors contributed to the success of the U.S. troop surge:

• Setting up joint U.S.-Iraqi security stations across Iraq in urban centers where troops could live and work near to vulnerable populations.

• Americans and Iraqis living together in the joint security stations and patrolling and, when necessary, fighting together in Iraq's toughest urban neighborhoods.

• Development of a campaign plan that was gradually passing more and more responsibility to Iraqis for all aspects of their country's governance.

• Prime Minister Nouri al-Maliki purging many Shi'a extremist leaders whom he considered irreconcilable, and replacing them, in many cases, with former Ba'athists (mostly Sunni) with whom he thought he could work. Iraqi and American leaders convinced Muqtada al-Sadr to agree to a ceasefire.

• The United States launched the so-called "Sons of Iraq" program, paying some of the very same tribesmen (generally Sunni) who had been part of the insurgency two years previously to cooperate with the Americans in providing security.

• While U.S. forces surged by 30,000 in 2007, Iraqi security forces grew by some 200,000 between 2005 and 2007. By the end of 2008, the U.S. total was more than 500,000 personnel.

BATTLE OF BASRA

In 2007, operations by Coalition and Iraqi forces made significant gains against al Qaeda and other Sunni insurgents in Iraq. As the threat from these groups decreased, Coalition forces and the Iraqi government focused their attention on the problem of Shi'a militias in central and southern Iraq. Nowhere was this threat more evident than in the southern city of Basra. In the wake of the British withdrawal from the city center and transition to an overwatch capacity in late 2007, Basra became a safe haven for militia and criminal activity. Rival Shi'a militias were engaged in a violent and protracted power struggle, as drugs, weapons, and oil smuggling rings thrived. In late March 2008, the Iraqi government launched a military offensive to reclaim the city from the militias. It was known as "Operation Knight's Charge."

U.S. troops on patrol near Basra. The offensive against the Shi'a militias in Basra in March 2008 strengthened the Iraqi government and showed terrorist groups that Iraq was no longer a safe haven for their activities.

BATTLE OF BASRA

Location   Basra, southern Iraq

Date   March 25-31, 2008

Commanders and forces   Iraqi Security Forces: 30,000 troops; Mahdi Army: 16,000 troops (Muqtada al-Sadr)

Casualties   Iraqi: 30 killed, 400 wounded; Mahdi Army: 400 killed, 600 wounded, 155 taken prisoner

Key actions   By the end of the first week, the offensive had reached a stalemate. In the face of Iranian-supported enemy resistance, the Iraqi Security Forces were unable to take control of the Jaysh al-Mahdi's heavily fortified neighborhood strongholds. The intense clashes continued, with neither side gaining momentum. An agreement between Muqtada al-Sadr and representatives from rival Shi'a parties, brokered in Iran by the head of the Islamic Revolutionary Guards Corps-Qods Force (IRGC-QF), calmed the violence in Basra at the end of March. On April 1, Iraqi Security Force reinforcements arrived in Basra and prepared for larger-scale clearing operations.

Key effects   The Basra offensive marked the first time that the Shi'a-led Iraqi government had seriously addressed the problem of Shi'a militias, namely Sadr's Jaysh al-Mahdi militia. Despite their shaky start, the Iraqi Security Forces, with important Coalition enablers, were able to reclaim vast areas of Basra from militia control. Moreover, the government of Iraq was able to reassert control of the economically vital ports and oil infrastructure, and Prime Minister Maliki was able to improve his standing as a decisive and powerful leader.

From 2001 the United States launched several major initiatives intended to remake the Middle East as part of the War on Terror. This included the overthrow of Saddam and the political reconstruction of Iraq; the "Road Map" proposal for Israeli-Palestinian peace; a "forward strategy" to encourage democracy in the region; multilateral efforts to contain nuclear proliferation; and a program to encourage economic growth. All told, it was the most ambitious policy ever attempted to transform the prospects of a region sunk in a generation of economic stagnation, religious turmoil, and violent conflicts.

Saudi Arabia

Saudi Arabia's two key political communities are the Westernizing technocrats, centered in Jeddah, and the Wahhabi clerics, who believe that all political associations should be based on religion, not national identity. There is no single Wahhabism, but the main line of interpretation began with Ibn Tayimiya, passed through his students, and was revived by Ibn Abdul Wahhab in the 18th century. Wahhab made common cause with the Saudi royal family and gave the dynasty its official ideology.

Saudi Arabia is currently in the throes of a population explosion. With half the population under the age of 20 and the economy declining, the younger generation knows it cannot hope to enjoy its parents' standard of living. It is therefore increasingly resentful, and both technocrats and clerics agree that something has got to give. But institutional change poses a big problem for the clerics, who own a large part of the state—schools, the judiciary, the police, and the mosques.

The Arab–Israeli issue remains a major problem. President Bush attempted to break the stalemate by publicly endorsing an independent Palestinian state, but coupling it to demands for Palestinian reform and

Smoke billows into the sky after an Israeli air-launched missile strikes a target in a southern suburb of the city of Beirut in Lebanon, Saturday July 15, 2006. Israeli warplanes launched their attack on Lebanon because the country was considered a safe haven for terrorists. The Israelis targeted bridges, fuel storage depots, and gas stations in the east and south of the city.

democracy. The U.S.-led "Road Map," developed by the "Quartet" of the U.S., European Union, Russia, and United Nations (UN), failed, however, when Palestinian leader Yassir Arafat sabotaged efforts to suppress terrorism by his first Prime Minister Abu Mazen. By late 2003, the process began to look like a dead end to Israelis, and Israeli Prime Minister Ariel Sharon adopted a new strategy of withdrawing or "disengaging" from Gaza unilaterally. This "unilateral" initiative turned out to be the most multilateral of all the initiatives, involving the Palestinians, Egyptians, Americans, and Europeans.

Arab countries and the War on Terror

After 9/11, Syria, Egypt, and Jordan condemned the attacks and offered assistance to the United States. None of them publicly condemned the war in Afghanistan. Their position shifted, however, in September 2002, when President Bush sought the UN's consent to make Iraq the second phase of the War on Terror, which all three opposed. Then they separated from each other, with Egypt and Jordan acceding to and even providing logistical help for the war while Syria continued to oppose it.

All three countries were hurt by the war economically, as they had benefited from both legal and illegal dealings with Iraq and depended on her for oil and trade (the U.S. did compensate Jordan for this loss). Politically, they shifted their focus from possible reform to regime survival in view of the Bush doctrine. For example, Jordan's King Abdullah restored the country's parliament and took other steps to satisfy the U.S., and continued to receive aid. Egypt did its best to retain regional influence and introduce those reforms it could short of democracy.

Syria, meanwhile, was the subject of the Syrian Accountability Act President Bush introduced in December 2003, which called for it to halt its support for groups such as Hamas and Hezbullah, cease developing biological and chemical weapons, withdraw its forces from Lebanon, cease interference in Iraq, and enter into negotiations with Israel. The act had limited effect and Syria continued to support terrorist groups in Lebanon and Gaza.

AL QAEDA IN EGYPT

The coffins of 36 victims of the terrorist massacre in Luxor, Egypt, in November 1997 are lined up in a Zurich airport hangar.

Experts say Osama bin Laden's terror network grew in part out of Egyptian extremist groups, when he brought two leaders of Egyptian Islamic Jihad, Ayman al-Zawahiri and the late Mohammad Atef, into the top echelons of al Qaeda. Zawahiri and EIJ extremists joined with bin Laden when they became the targets of Egyptian anti-terrorism campaigns. EIJ members are known for their militancy and their specialty skills with weapons and strategic military planning, according to the *New York Times*, making them ideal recruits to al Qaeda. The EIJ received most of its funding from al Qaeda from 1998, and the groups merged in June 2001.

Many experts think that Atef and Zawahiri, who had been jailed in Egypt for his part in President Sadat's 1981 assassination, were behind al Qaeda's attacks on U.S. embassies in East Africa in 1998 and the 9/11 attacks (Atef was reported killed in a U.S. bombing raid in Afghanistan shortly after September 11).

EGYPTIAN ISLAMIC JIHAD

Egyptian Islamic Jihad (EIJ), a militant Islamist group that emerged in the 1970s, changed its focus in 2001. Originally bent on installing a religious government in Egypt, the group joined forces with Osama bin Laden's al Qaeda network that year and broadened its aims. Largely absorbed into al Qaeda, EIJ opposes Western influence in the Muslim world, including those Arab governments that are aligned with Washington, rails against secularism generally, and regularly denounces Israel, the United States, and governments that support either. According to the 2007 State Department Country Reports on Terrorism, EIJ has been active worldwide "for several years under the auspices" of al Qaeda. EIJ is thought to be involved with most of the terrorist attacks on the United States in the last two decades, and its operatives played a key role in both attacks on the World Trade Center. Like Jamaat al-Islamiyya, some EIJ members were once members of the mainstream Muslim Brotherhood, but broke with that group over its commitment to nonviolence. Members of EIJ and Jamaat fought alongside the Afghan mujahideen in the 1980s war opposing Soviet occupation, as well as in Yemen's long-running civil war.

THE POSITION OF IRAN

Since a 1979 revolution led by Ayatollah Khomeini toppled the U.S.-backed regime of Shah Mohammad Reza Pahlavi, Iran has been governed by Shi'a Muslim clerics committed to a strict interpretation of Islamic law. Supreme leader Ayatollah Ali Khamenei now serves as commander-in-chief of the military and police force. He is also the head of Islamic Republic of Iran Broadcasting (IRIB), the state ministry in control of television and radio, and the leader of the country's judiciary. Other top leaders include Ali Larijani, leader of the Supreme National Security Council (SNSC), and Mahmoud Ahmadinejad, Iran's elected president, who has aroused controversy by calling for Israel's elimination. However, his power is checked by Larijani.

In 2005, Ali Larijani, told *Agence France Presse* that Iran had extradited all foreign members of al Qaeda and tried any Iranian suspects. U.S. officials say Iran mostly backs Shi'a Islamist groups, including the Lebanese militants of Hezbullah and the Palestinian terrorist groups Hamas and Palestinian Islamic Jihad. A few months after Hamas won the Palestinian Authority (PA) elections in 2006, Iran pledged $50 million to the near-bankrupt PA. The United States, among other nations, has cut off aid to the PA because of Hamas' terrorist ties.

Iran is suspected of encouraging Hezbullah's 2006 attack on Israel to deflect attention from its nuclear weapons program. Reports also suggest that Iran's interference in Iraq has included funding, safe transit for militants, and arms to insurgent leaders such as Muqtada al-Sadr and his forces.

IRAN AND IRAQ

The Quds Force, a special operations wing of Iran's Revolutionary Guard Corps, is accused by U.S. officials of furnishing Shi'a militias with explosively formed penetrators (EFPs), or roadside bombs, as well as rocket-propelled grenades and Katyusha rockets. Specifically, the United States alleges that it supports, trains, and finances militias such as the Badr Brigade, the armed wing of one of Iraq's most religious Shi'ite parties, whose base is in southern Iraq. "The Quds Force is to the Shi'a militias as al Qaeda in Iraq is to the Sunni insurgent groups," writes Rick Francona, a retired military intelligence official and former U.S. Air Force lieutenant colonel. Some experts estimate as many as 30,000 Iranian operatives may be in Iraq. In October 2007, the U.S. State Department designated the Revolutionary Guard and the Quds Force supporters of terrorism, and imposed sweeping economic sanctions on both of these groups.

Saudi-born al Qaeda leader Osama bin Laden has long called for the overthrow of the Saudi royal family to punish it for allowing the establishment of U.S. military bases in the kingdom. He finally broke with the monarchy in 1990 over the Persian Gulf War, when the kingdom invited U.S.-led Coalition troops onto Saudi soil to defend its oil fields and to prepare for the invasion of Iraqi-held Kuwait. After the fall of Saddam Hussein's regime in the Second Iraq War, U.S. troops pulled out of Saudi Arabia.

Osama bin Laden's al Qaeda is targeting the Saudi kingdom for several reasons. The royal family maintains a close relationship with the United States, which al Qaeda views as the home of "infidels." Many Saudis see the powerful princes who run the country as corrupt and dissolute. In this view, the royals are leaders of a strict Islamic state who disregard Islam's principles by drinking alcohol or frequenting the casinos of Monte Carlo. Al Qaeda regards the regime as insufficiently Islamic and an unacceptable guardian of Mecca and Medina, Islam's holiest sites. In addition, some experts say, the government is breaking its social

contract with Saudi citizens, which gives the royal family control over politics in exchange for lifetime benefits financed by Saudi oil.

Al Qaeda is not the only Islamist group in the country. Sahwa (Awakening) was founded in the 1990s as a grassroots movement against secularism. Where al Qaeda promotes violent Jihad, Sahwa shuns any conflict that would it believes jeopardize what Muslims already have in Saudi Arabia.

MAJOR AL QAEDA ATTACKS

May 12, 2003: 34 people killed in a series of bomb attacks in Riyadh.

May 29-30, 2004: Gunmen attack offices in the city of Khobar, killing a number of people.

June 18, 2004: Militants behead U.S. engineer Paul Johnson after holding him hostage for a week.

December 6, 2004: Nine people are killed in an attack on the U.S. consulate in Jeddah, Saudi Arabia.

The main al Qaeda bases throughout the Middle East. Each base operates its own group of fighters and can act independently or in cooperation with other bases.

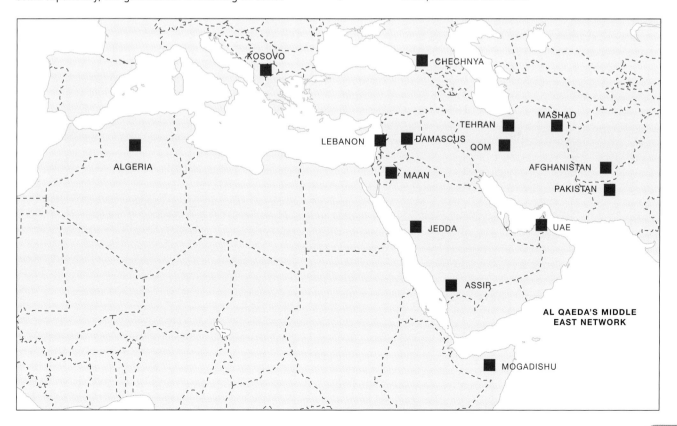

AL QAEDA'S MIDDLE EAST NETWORK

Between 1982 and 2000, Israel occupied Lebanon's southern strip to create a security zone south of the Litani River, 13 miles (21 km) from the Lebanese–Israeli border, in order to halt the firing of Katyusha rockets into Israeli territory. On July 12, 2006, Hezbullah crossed the blue line demarcated by the United Nations (UN) in 2000, killing eight Israeli soldiers and kidnapping two others. In retaliation, Israel invaded Lebanon.

In the war that followed there was from a military perspective no decisive battle, no decisive winner, and no clear loser. In the air and rocket war, Israel's air force scored important victories against Hezbullah's long- and medium-range rockets, but had no answer to the short-range Katyushas. Hezbullah continued to bombard northern Israel throughout the conflict.

On August 11, 2006, the United Nations Security Council unanimously approved UN Resolution 1701, in an effort to end the hostilities. The resolution, which was approved by both Lebanese and Israeli governments in the following days, called for the disarmament of Hezbullah, the withdrawal of Israeli forces from Lebanon, and the deployment of Lebanese soldiers in combination with an enlarged United Nations Interim Force in Lebanon (UNIFIL) force in southern Lebanon. As a result of the UN Resolution, the Lebanese Army began deploying into southern Lebanon on August 17, 2006.

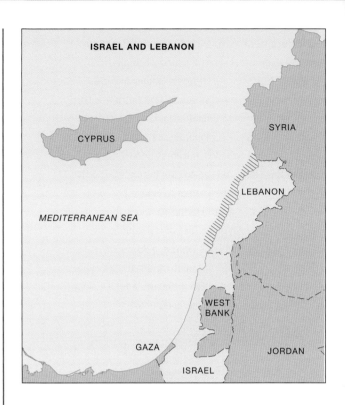

ISRAEL'S WAR ON HEZBULLAH

Location Southern Lebanon

Date July 12–August 14, 2006

Commanders and forces Israel: 30,000 troops (General Dan Halutz); Hezbullah: 15,000 fighters (Hassan Nasrallah)

Casualties Israel: 121 killed, 628 wounded; Hezbullah: 250 killed

Key actions July 25: The Battle of Bint Jbeil was one of the main actions of the war. It consisted of a series of military engagements in the southern Lebanese town of Bint Jbeil, regarded as a Hezbullah stronghold of the south.

Key effects The war brought into international focus the role of Iran as a destabilizing force in the region (it provided rockets to Hezbullah). The fear of Iranian regional ascendancy brought together an unusual group of states in publicly blaming Hezbullah for recklessness in provoking the war. It is unprecedented for three Sunni Arab states—Saudi Arabia, Egypt, and Jordan—to charge another Arab party with instigating a confrontation with Israel. These states understand that Iran has backed militias in Iraq, Gaza, and Lebanon, and they fear this recipe for instability could spread in the Middle East in the coming years.

FATAH–HAMAS CONFLICT

The Palestinian Authority (PA) and Fatah, its main constituent body, lost popular support through corruption. Into this void stepped Hamas. Although it rejects democracy, Hamas participated in the elections to the Palestinian parliament in January 2006 and won a majority of seats. Subsequently, Hamas formed a government with Isma'il Haniyeh as prime minister. Fatah subsequently refused to turn over public funds and control of the armed forces to Hamas.

Hamas is allied with Hezbullah and with various al Qaeda groups acting as proxies of Iran and Syria. Some alliances seem improbable: Hamas, a Sunni movement, is allied with the Shi'a Hezbullah, and acts as a proxy for Shi'a Iran and for the Syrian Ba'ath regime, which suppresses the Muslim Brotherhood in Syria.

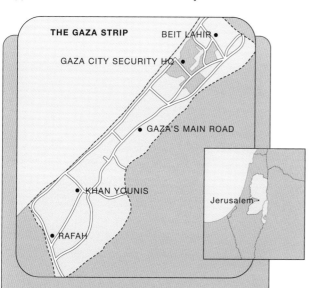

FATAH–HAMAS CONFLICT

Location   Gaza, Middle East

Date   December 15, 2006–present

Commanders and forces   Hamas: 15,000 fighters (Isma'il Haniyeh); Fatah: 50,000 fighters (Mahmoud Abbas)

Casualties   Hamas (to 2008): 83 killed; Fatah (to 2008): 165 killed

Key actions   On June 12, 2007, Hamas fighters surrounded the headquarters of Fatah in Gaza, where 500 Fatah fighters were holed up. The Hamas militants attacked the building and, after several hours of intense fighting, took control of the headquarters. In addition, several other Fatah positions were overrun throughout the Gaza Strip. Fighting was reported to have taken place in at least two hospitals. By the end of the day, the towns of Beit Lahir and Rafah were under Hamas control.

Key effects   The clashes led to the collapse of the PA in Gaza. The PA's security forces were easily beaten by armed units of Hamas, and PA forces surrendered or disappeared. The PA Fatah leadership fled to Ramalla.

FATAH AL-ISLAM IN LEBANON

Citizens celebrate after the Lebanese Army cleared the streets of Tripoli of militant fighters from the Palestinian Fatah al-Islam group in May 2007.

Fatah al-Islam is a militant Sunni Islamist group said to have Lebanese, Syrian, and Palestinian members. Reuters reports that it began with 200 members, yet militants from other Palestinian groups have since joined. It is also reported to have ties to al Qaeda. Based in Lebanon, it gained notoriety in May 2007 after clashes with Lebanese security forces left dozens of people dead. Many in Lebanon view Fatah al-Islam as a fringe group with no popular backing. As Fatah al-Islam drew the Lebanese Army into a protracted conflict, these Lebanese complained that the country had been hijacked by extremists.

On May 20, 2007, a battle between Fatah al-Islam and Lebanese troops left at least 41 dead. The fighting began when Lebanese security forces investigating a bank robbery raided an apartment north of Tripoli. In response, Fatah al-Islam seized control of army posts at the Nahr al-Bared refugee camp, which Lebanese tanks then proceeded to shell. The camp's electricity, phone lines, and water were cut off. On-and-off fighting continued for weeks, leaving scores dead or wounded.

THE AL QAEDA LINK

Syria claims that Fatah al-Islam is connected to al Qaeda, while Lebanon says the group was sent by Damascus to destabilize Lebanon and has no ties to al Qaeda. While most Lebanese Sunni Islamists are not linked to al Qaeda and the group has no organizational or logistical links to al Qaeda, it does subscribe to Osama bin Laden's ideology of war against non-Muslims—specifically the West—and its goal of replacing the governments of Muslim countries with fundamentalist Islamic regimes. Following Fatah al-Islam's initial clashes with the Lebanese Army, al Qaeda leaders called on Muslims to support the group.

Throughout Asia there are terrorist organizations, insurgents, and revolutionaries of many different kinds. What sets apart the terrorist groups that are operating in Southeast Asia is the intimate cooperation among them. Although insurgent groups in Southeast Asia's terrorist brotherhood do not share the same goals, their cooperation across national boundaries creates an economy of scale for logistics, training, and for the establishment of safe havens. For example, Jemaah Islamiyah (JI) and the Free Aceh Movement (GAM) have trained with the Moro Islamic Liberation Front (MILF) in camps that are located in the southern Philippines; GAM smuggles weapons with the Thai terrorist group Pattani United Liberation Organization (PULO); and many terrorists use regional connections to move from country to country. Jemaah Islamiyah, which is based in Indonesia and has operated in the Philippines, has traditionally had particularly strong ties to al Qaeda. Abu Sayyaf, whose name means "bearer of the sword" in Arabic, is a militant organization based in the southern Philippines. It seeks to establish a separate Islamic state for the country's Muslim minority. The White House says Abu Sayyaf is a terrorist organization that boasts of its ties to Osama bin Laden's al Qaeda network.

Intelligence failures

Many groups within Southeast Asia's terrorist brotherhood, such as GAM, PULO, Gerakan Mujahideen Islam Pattani (GMIP), Kampulan Militan Malaysia (KMM), Majelis Mujahidin Indonesia (MMI), Laskar Jihad, Indonesian Islamic Liberation Front (IILF), and the MILF, do not appear on the U.S. State Department's or on the United Nations' list of Foreign Terrorist Organizations (FTO). This oversight has implications for the effectiveness of antiterrorist strategies in the region, because current policies attack only a portion of the terrorist network.

Recent developments in the war on terrorism have made Asia—and in particular Southeast Asia—central to

Rebels of the Moro Islamic Liberation Front (MILF) stand in formation during a show of force at Camp Darapanan, Maguindanao, southern Philippines. The group is believed to have links with al Qaeda.

the U.S. strategy to defeat terrorism. National Security Advisor Condoleezza Rice described Southeast Asia as "a very important front" in the war on terrorism, because it poses a serious threat to economic prosperity as well as political stability.

Although terrorists in Southeast Asia work closely together, regional governments often do not. Several countries in Southeast Asia have made considerable individual progress combating terrorism, yet cooperation and coordination among Southeast Asian states is generally sporadic. The terrorist brotherhood continues to take advantage of this poor regional cooperation to hide from authorities simply by moving to the country next door.

The weaknesses of local governments

Terrorist groups have exploited this weakness, seeking refuge where local authorities are least committed to countering terrorism—notably in Indonesia and the Philippines. Although Indonesian officials argue that there is enough political will to crackdown on Jemaah Islamiyah, Southeast Asia's major Islamist terror network, convicted terrorists have received light sentences. Former Indonesian President Megawati Sukarnoputri did not deal with the militant Islamic religious schools that have been a major source of JI recruitment. Susilo Bambang Yudhoyono, who was elected president in 2004, outlawed JI in 2005. The weak legal system that operates in Indonesia, however, hardly helps the situation.

The Filipino government may be the weakest link in Southeast Asia's antiterrorist efforts. Although there have been hundreds of terrorist arrests since the Bali bombings of 2002, disproportionately few have occurred in the Philippines. There is almost no mechanism to effectively enforce the law, because there are more soldiers in the country than police. Furthermore, there is no coastguard or maritime police force in place to control borders that are weakened by corruption. Finally, the continuing existence of a terrorist haven in Mindanao in the southern Philippines, unmolested by government security forces, permits Southeast Asia's terrorist brotherhood to plan and train for their next attacks.

U.S aid: Master Sgt. Joseph Salvador, U.S. Air Force, explains emergency equipment to members of the Philippine Air Force.

The U.S. State Department has seen the southern Philippines as a "terrorist safe haven" since 2006. U.S. officials say that the Philippine government has little control there, where resentment has grown among the Muslim minority over government policies.

The major terrorist groups in the Philippines are: the Abu Sayyaf Group, the Communist Party of the Philippines/New People's Army, Jemaah Islamiyah, and the Moro Islamic Liberation Front (MILF). MILF has an estimated armed strength of 10,000. Experts say al Qaeda's influence appears to be channeled through Jemaah Islamiyah and the Abu Sayyaf Group, and that al Qaeda's presence has professionalized local groups and forged ties among them, so that they can better cooperate. In many cases, this cooperation has taken the form of ad hoc arrangements of convenience, such as helping to procure weapons and explosives.

Jemaah Islamiyah (JI) is a militant Islamist group active in several Southeast Asian countries. It seeks to establish a pan-Islamic state across much of the region. Antiterrorist authorities struck a blow against Jemaah Islamiyah ("Islamic Organization" in Arabic) when they arrested its operational chief, Nurjaman Riduan Ismuddin, also known as Hambali, in Thailand in 2003. More recently, authorities in Jakarta arrested JI's leader, Abu Dujana, in June 2007. JI is alleged to have attacked or plotted against U.S. and Western targets in Indonesia, Singapore, and the Philippines.

Experts refer to JI as al Qaeda's Southeast Asian wing, while others argue the two are not that closely linked and add that Jemaah Islamiyah's regional goals do not fully match al Qaeda's global aspirations. Abu Bakar Bashir, JI's alleged spiritual leader, denies the group has ties to al Qaeda, but has expressed support for Osama bin Laden. An al Qaeda operative arrested in Indonesia reportedly told U.S. investigators that Bashir was directly involved in al Qaeda plots.

However, a few individuals have been linked to both groups. Hambali is the Jemaah Islamiyah leader thought to be most closely linked to al Qaeda. He has allegedly been involved in several terrorist attacks in the region. Some say he delegated responsibilities while being pursued by Indonesian and other intelligence services. Others with suspected ties to al Qaeda and Jemaah Islamiyah have been detained in the region, and some have been turned over to U.S. investigators.

U.S. AID

Since 2001, U.S. forces have engaged in many counterterrorism exercises with the Philippine military. In 2006 alone, the United States and the Philippines scheduled up to 37 joint exercises. Most notable is the annual Balikatan ("shoulder-to-shoulder") bilateral exercises, which the U.S. State Department says, "contribute directly to the Philippine armed forces' efforts to root out Abu Sayyaf and Jemaah Islamiyah terrorists." The U.S. State and Defense departments also reward informants in the Philippines when their information leads directly to the capture or killing of suspected terrorists. In 2007, the United States paid out more than $10 million for intelligence leading to the arrest or killing of 13 alleged members of Abu Sayyaf. U.S. prosecutors and FBI agents have also provided training to 34 representatives of the Philippine Anti-Terrorism Council. The United States has helped the Philippines establish interagency intelligence centers to support maritime interdictions against transnational criminal/terrorist organizations and a "Coast Watch" system in Mindanao.

PIRACY AND TERRORISM

The newest terrorist target may be global shipping. Southeast Asia, where the rate of maritime piracy is already the worst in the world, is particularly vulnerable to maritime terrorism. In 2004 Lloyd's of London reported that terrorists might be training maritime pilots in the Malacca Straits to capture a ship, pilot it into a port or chokepoint, and detonate it. The strategic shipping route between Indonesia's Sumatra island and the Southeast Asian peninsula of Malaysia and Singapore was deemed the most dangerous waterway in the world in 2005. The Malacca sea-lane carries about 40 percent of the world's trade, including a major part of the energy imports of China and Japan. However, unlike the pirate-infested Gulf of Aden off the coast of Somalia, the nations of the Southeast Asian region have relatively well-organized maritime police forces and navies, supported by backing from allies such as the United States. U.S. aid for Indonesia's antipiracy efforts includes 15 high-speed response boats, some of which are based at Batam opposite Singapore at the most vulnerable chokepoint in the Malacca Straits. In 2008, there were only two pirate attacks in the straits, compared to 38 in 2004 and down from a peak of 75 in 2000.

2002 BALI BOMBING

The 2002 Bali terrorist bombings are sometimes called "Australia's September 11" because of the large number of Australians killed in the attack. It took place in the town of Kuta on the Indonesian island of Bali. Just after 23:00 hours on October 12, 2002, a bomb hidden in a backpack exploded inside a popular tourist destination, Paddy's Bar. The device killed the backpack owner, suspected of being a suicide operative.

Approximately 10–15 seconds later, a second, more powerful car bomb, of close to 2,200 lb (1,000 kg), concealed in a white Mitsubishi van, was detonated by remote control in front of the Sari Club. The explosion left a 3-ft (1-m) deep crater, and windows throughout the town were blown out. A third bomb was then detonated in the street in front of the U.S. consulate in Bali. This bomb caused a slight injury to one person, and only modest damage. However, it was packed with excrement for maximum moral outrage.

As the local hospital was unable to cope with the number of injured, particularly burns victims, many of the wounded of all nationalities were flown by the Royal Australian Air Force to hospitals in Darwin and other Australian cities. In total, Jemaah Islamiyah had killed 202 people and injured a further 209.

THE 2005 BOMBINGS

In 2005, Jemaah Islamiyah struck again in Bali, with a series of terrorist suicide bomb attacks on October 1, 2005. Bombs exploded at two sites in Jimbaran and Kuta, both in south Bali. Twenty people were killed, and 129 people were injured by three bombers, who killed themselves in the attacks. It was a timely reminder that Indonesia has the largest Muslim population in the world, which, combined with rampant poverty and political instability, could fuel the growth of al Qaeda-linked terrorist cells.

Indonesian police officers among wrecked cars at the site of the terrorist bomb blasts in Kuta, Bali, on October 12, 2002. Around 200 people were killed in attacks in the popular tourist center.

ATTACK ON THE AUSTRALIAN EMBASSY

The Australian flag flies next to the ruins of the country's embassy in Jakart, Indonesia, after the terrorist attack of September 2004.

The 2004 Australian embassy bombing took place on September 9, 2004, in Jakarta, Indonesia. A large bomb, packed into a small Daihatsu delivery van, exploded outside the Australian embassy in Kuningan District, South Jakarta, at about 10:30 hours, killing nine people including the suicide bomber, and wounding 150 others. It gutted the Greek embassy on the 12th floor of an adjacent building, where three diplomats were slightly wounded. Damage to the nearby Chinese embassy was reported and numerous other office buildings in the vicinity were also damaged by the blast, which shattered windows in buildings 500 yards (450 m) away, injuring many workers inside, mostly by broken glass. The attack was the work of Islamic terrorists, led by Noordin Mohammed Top.

ANZUS

The United States–Australia strategic and defense relationship, under the rubric of the Australia–New Zealand–United States (ANZUS) alliance, remains extremely close. Australian access to intelligence and U.S. arms are key aspects of the bilateral relationship. A long-standing treaty ally, Australia has fought alongside the United States in most of America's wars and established a Free Trade Agreement with the United States in 2005. In September 2007, the nations signed the Australia–United States Treaty on Defense Trade Cooperation, that is intended to ease restrictions associated with the International Trade in Arms Regulations (ITAR) by creating a comprehensive framework within which most defense trade can be carried out without prior government approval. Despite these ties, the relationship faces diplomatic recalibration. Prime Minister John Howard, a staunch supporter of Bush administration policies, was defeated in parliamentary elections in November 2007. His replacement, Kevin Rudd of the Labor Party, while recognizing the constructive role that the United States plays in underpinning security in the Asia Pacific region, as well as the centrality of the ANZUS alliance to Australian security interests, has distanced himself from some aspects of U.S. policy.

THAILAND

Since 2004, an insurgency by militants in Thailand's southern, predominantly Muslim, provinces has claimed a total of nearly 3,000 lives. The Thai military imposed martial law in the insurgent provinces in January 2004. However, the Thai government and its military forces showed no real signs of being able to decisively defeat the insurgency.

The main terrorist groups involved in this revolt against the Thai authorities are:

• Barisan Revolusi Nasional-Coordinate (BRN-C). Possibly the largest and most well organized of the separatist groups, the BRN-C is the only active faction of an organization founded in the early 1960s to fight for an independent, religious state. The group recruits members from Islamic schools.
• Pattani United Liberation Organization (PULO). Part of a second wave of more secular separatist groups, this guerrilla organization was established in 1968. A splinter group known as New PULO split from the main organization in 1995, but the two factions allied again two years later. Most of its leaders are based abroad.
• Bersatu. An umbrella organization of various southern terrorist groups, Bersatu was founded in 1989. The coalition counts PULO and BRN-C among its members. This merger may have resulted from their weakening during the 1980s.
• Gerakan Mujahidin Islam Pattani (GMIP). Established in part by Afghan veterans in 1995 in order to support a separate Islamic state, GMIP almost certainly has connections to a Malaysian counterpart called Kumpulan Mujahideen Malay.

THAILAND AND THE WAR ON TERROR

The insurgency in Thailand has important implications for the United States, as Bangkok is a long-term military ally in the war against terrorism in Southeast Asia and a significant trade and economic partner. Thailand also contributed troops and support for U.S. military operations in both Afghanistan and Iraq, and was designated as a major non-NATO ally by President George W. Bush in December 2003. Its airfields and ports play a significant role in U.S. global military strategy, including having served as the primary hub of the relief effort following the 2004 Indian Ocean tsunami. The insurgency's potential to expand in the future poses a threat to U.S. strategic interests in the region.

The war on terror in Southeast Asia is going well. JI is to all intents and purposes decimated. In this respect, the "war" in Southeast Asia has essentially been won. This being the case, Europe is today the second front. Southeast Asia is by comparison a distant third.

The "war on terror" did not receive much response from several countries in the region. It hardly appeared on the political radar in Myanmar, Laos, Vietnam, and Brunei. In countries such as Malaysia, which has zero tolerance for terrorism of any kind and which disabled JI elements there promptly, it was never the nation's main security threat. For Myanmar, Thailand, and the Philippines, the biggest threats came from domestic insurgencies and not from international terrorism. These domestic insurgencies had existed well before September 11. The insurgencies that claimed most attention involved Buddhists in Myanmar, Muslims who were opposing the Thai government in Thailand, and Catholic and Muslim insurgents who were fighting the Manila government in the Philippines. The priorities of the United States were not shared here.

NOORDIN MOHAMMED TOP

Noordin Mohammed Top is Southeast Asia's most wanted terrorist. For the Australian embassy bombing in September 2004, he relied on three networks: the East Java division of Jemaah Islamiyah (JI); alumni of JI schools in Central Java; and a West Java-based faction of an old insurgency, Darul Islam, whose members supplied the key operatives. While individuals from that Ring Banten faction had worked with JI before, military operations had never before been outsourced in this way. It was one indication that Noordin was working on his own. He continues to wage Jihad against the U.S. and its allies on Indonesian soil.

Guerrilla fighters of the New People's Army display their weapons at a secret jungle base in the Philippines in 1987.

THE UNITED STATES

On **September 20, 2001,** President George W. Bush gave the following address to a Joint Session of Congress and to the American people. It contains the guiding principles of what would become the War on Terror: the military, political, legal, and ideological conflict against Islamic terrorism:

"On September 11th, enemies of freedom committed an act of war against our country. Americans have known wars—but for the past 136 years, they have been wars on foreign soil, except for one Sunday in 1941. Americans have known the casualties of war—but not at the center of a great city on a peaceful morning. Americans have known surprise attacks—but never before on thousands of civilians. All of this was brought upon us in a single day—and night fell on a different world, a world where freedom itself is under attack.

Identifying the enemy

"Americans have many questions tonight. Americans are asking: Who attacked our country? The evidence we have gathered all points to a collection of loosely affiliated terrorist organizations known as al Qaeda. They are the same murderers indicted for bombing American embassies in Tanzania and Kenya, and responsible for bombing the USS *Cole*.

"Al Qaeda is to terror what the Mafia is to crime. But its goal is not making money; its goal is remaking the world—and imposing its radical beliefs on people everywhere. The terrorists practice a fringe form of Islamic extremism that has been rejected by Muslim scholars and the vast majority of Muslim clerics—a fringe movement that perverts the peaceful teachings of Islam. The terrorists' directive commands them to kill Christians and Jews, to kill all Americans, and make no distinction among military and civilians, including women and children.

"This group and its leader—a person named Osama bin Laden—are linked to many other organizations in different countries, including the

President Bush gives his address to a Joint Session of Congress and the American people on September 20, 2001.

Egyptian Islamic Jihad and the Islamic Movement of Uzbekistan. There are thousands of these terrorists in more than 60 countries. They are recruited from their own nations and neighborhoods and brought to camps in places like Afghanistan, where they are trained in the tactics of terror. They are sent back to their homes or sent to hide in countries around the world to plot evil and destruction.

"The leadership of al Qaeda has great influence in Afghanistan and supports the Taliban regime in controlling most of that country. In Afghanistan, we see al Qaeda's vision for the world. Afghanistan's people have been brutalized—many are starving and many have fled. Women are not allowed to attend school. You can be jailed for owning a television. Religion can be practiced only as their leaders dictate. A man can be jailed in Afghanistan if his beard is not long enough.

The weaknesses of local governments

"The United States respects the people of Afghanistan—after all, we are currently its largest source of humanitarian aid—but we condemn the Taliban regime. It is not only repressing its own people, it is threatening people everywhere by sponsoring and sheltering and supplying terrorists. By aiding and abetting murder, the Taliban regime is committing murder. Our war on terror begins with al Qaeda, but it does not end there. It will not end until every terrorist group of global reach has been found, stopped and defeated. The course of this conflict is not known, yet its outcome is certain. Freedom and fear, justice and cruelty, have always been at war, and we know that God is not neutral between them.

"Fellow citizens, we'll meet violence with patient justice—assured of the rightness of our cause, and confident of the victories to come. In all that lies before us, may God grant us wisdom, and may He watch over the United States of America.

Thank you."

Thus did the United States become the driving force behind the War on Terror, determined to defeat terrorists and destroy their organizations. It is a war that is still ongoing.

STRATEGIC GOALS

A U.S. Air Force F-15E Strike Eagle launches heat decoys during a close-air-support mission over Afghanistan.

Since the terrorist attacks of September 11, 2001, the United States has initiated three military operations:

1) Operation Enduring Freedom (OEF), covering Afghanistan and other War on Terror operations, from the Philippines to Djibouti, which began immediately after the 9/11 attacks and continues;

2) Operation Noble Eagle (ONE), providing enhanced security for U.S. military bases and other homeland security, which was launched in response to the attacks and continues at a modest level; and

3) Operation Iraqi Freedom (OIF) which began in the fall of 2002, with the buildup of troops for the March 2003 invasion of Iraq, and continues with counter-insurgency and stability operations.

The cost of these operations is massive and has placed great strains on the U.S. economy (see below).

THE COST OF THE WAR ON TERROR

To 2008, the U.S. Congress had approved a total of about $864 billion for military operations, base security, reconstruction, foreign aid, embassy costs, and veterans' health care for the three operations initiated since the 9/11 attacks: "Operation Enduring Freedom" (OEF), Afghanistan and other counter terror operations; "Operation Noble Eagle" (ONE), providing enhanced security at military bases; and "Operation Iraqi Freedom" (OIF).

This $864 billion total covers all war-related costs from 2001 through part of 2009 in supplementals, regular appropriations, and continuing resolutions.

Of the total, Iraq received about $657 billion (76 percent), OEF about $173 billion (20 percent), and enhanced base security about $28 billion (3 percent), with about $5 billion for miscellaneous items (1 percent). About 94 percent of the funds were for the Department of Defense, 6 percent for foreign aid programs and embassy operations, and less than 1 percent for medical care for veterans.

THE PATRIOT ACT

Congress passed the USA Patriot Act in response to the terrorist attacks of September 11, 2001. The Act improves counterterrorism by the following measures:

• Allows law enforcement to use surveillance against more crimes of terror;
• Allows federal agents to follow sophisticated terrorists trained to evade detection;
• Allows law enforcement to conduct investigations without tipping off terrorists;
• Allows federal agents to seek court orders to obtain business records in national security terrorism cases;
• Allows law enforcement officials to obtain a search warrant anywhere a terrorist-related activity occurred;
• Allows victims of computer hacking to request law enforcement assistance in monitoring the "trespassers" on their computers;

The Patriot Act also increased the penalties for those who commit and support terrorist crimes. In particular, the Patriot Act:
• Prohibits the harboring of terrorists;
• Enhances the inadequate maximum penalties for various crimes likely to be committed by terrorists;
• Enhances conspiracy penalties, including for arson, killings in federal facilities, attacking communications, material support to terrorists, sabotage of nuclear facilities, and interference with flight crew members;
• Punishes terrorist attacks on mass transit systems;
• Punishes bioterrorists;
• Eliminates the statutes of limitations for certain terrorism crimes and also lengthens them for other terrorist crimes.

CONTROVERSIAL MEASURES

The Patriot Act includes the following controversial measures:
• The authorization of "roving wiretaps," so that law enforcement officials can get court orders to wiretap any phone a suspected terrorist might use. The provision was needed, advocates said, because of the advent of cellular and disposable phones.
• Permitting the federal government to detain non-U.S. citizens suspected of terrorism for up to seven days without specific charges. The U.S. administration originally wanted to hold them indefinitely.
Many feared that such powers gave the state too much power, and infringed on personal liberty—the very thing that the war on terror was supposed to protect.

DEPARTMENT OF HOMELAND SECURITY

HOMELAND SECURITY

Established: November 25, 2002

Headquarters: Nebraska Avenue Complex, Washington

Employees: 208,000 (2007)

Annual Budget: $52.0 billion (2009)

The following 22 agencies were incorporated into the new department:

U.S. Customs Service–Treasury

U.S. Coast Guard–Transportation

U.S. Secret Service–Treasury

United States Citizenship and Immigration Service (formerly Immigration and Naturalization Service)–Justice

U.S. Immigration and Customs Enforcement (formerly Immigration and Naturalization Service)–Justice

United States Federal Protective Service (part of ICE)

Transportation Security Administration–Transportation

Federal Law Enforcement Training Center–Treasury

Animal and Plant Health Inspection Service–Agriculture

Office for Domestic Preparedness–Justice

Federal Emergency Management Agency

Strategic National Stockpile and the National Disaster Medical System–HHS

Nuclear Incident Response Team–Energy

Domestic Emergency Support Teams–Justice

National Domestic Preparedness Office–FBI

CBRN Countermeasures Programs–Energy

Environmental Measurements Laboratory–Energy

National BW Defense Analysis Center–Defense

Plum Island Animal Disease Center–Agriculture

Federal Computer Incident Response Center–GSA

National Communications System–Defense

National Infrastructure Protection Center–FBI

Energy Security and Assurance Program–Energy

The Department of Homeland Security was approved by Congress in November 2002. It is designed to consolidate U.S. defenses against terrorist attack and to better coordinate counterterrorism intelligence. The department was established to absorb several federal agencies dealing with domestic defense, including the Coast Guard, the Border Patrol, the Customs Service, the Immigration and Naturalization Service, the Secret Service, and the Transportation Security Administration (which was created after September 11, 2001, to oversee airline security). Its responsibilities include exploring ways to respond to terror attacks and working to better coordinate intelligence about terrorist threats. The department is also expected to implement much of the National Strategy for Homeland Security, the domestic security plan unveiled by President Bush in July 2002.

Keeping the homeland safe from terrorism: two F-16 Fighting Falcons begin to roll into position over San Francisco for a rapid descent during an Operation Noble Eagle training patrol.

During his January 2002 State of the Union speech, President George W. Bush claimed that Iraq, Iran, and North Korea were in the process of developing weapons of mass destruction. Bush stated: "North Korea is a regime arming with missiles and weapons of mass destruction, while starving its citizens. Iran aggressively pursues these weapons and exports terror, while an unelected few repress the Iranian people's hope for freedom. Iraq continues to flaunt its hostility toward America and to support terror. The Iraqi regime has plotted to develop anthrax, and nerve gas, and nuclear weapons for over a decade. This is a regime that has already used poison gas to murder thousands of its own citizens—leaving the bodies of mothers huddled over their dead children. This is a regime that agreed to international inspections—then kicked out the inspectors. This is a regime that has something to hide from the civilized world."

NORTH KOREAN NUCLEAR WEAPONS

North Korea has only undertaken one test of a nuclear device. This test took place on October 9, 2006, and occurred after Pyongyang withdrew from the Treaty on the Nonproliferation of Nuclear Weapons (NPT) in January of 2003. Six-Party Talks between North Korea, South Korea, Japan, China, Russia, and the United States began in 2003 to quell North Korea's nuclear ambitions. However, the talks had broken down by 2005, leading ultimately to the 2006 nuclear test. The Six-Party Talks resumed and, in 2007, two milestone agreements were reached that called for the DPRK to shut down, seal, and disable its nuclear facility at Yongbyon in exchange for a total of one million tons of heavy fuel oil. Furthermore, North Korea agreed to provide a "complete and correct" declaration of all its nuclear facilities. On July 14, 2007, the IAEA confirmed that the Yongbyon nuclear facility had been shut down and sealed. Furthermore, on June 26, 2008, North Korea handed over its nuclear declaration and the disablement process at Yongbyon neared completion.

The CIA (Central Intelligence Agency) is responsible for providing national security intelligence to senior U.S. policymakers, with the following core aims:
• Collecting, correlating, and evaluating intelligence related to the national security and providing appropriate dissemination of such intelligence;
• Providing direction for and coordination of the collection of intelligence outside the United States;
• Performing other functions related to intelligence affecting the national security as the President or the Director of National Intelligence may direct.

The CIA is divided into four separate components: the National Clandestine Service, the Directorate of Intelligence, the Directorate of Science & Technology, and the Directorate of Support.

SUPPORT TO MILITARY OPERATIONS

One of the highest priorities for intelligence support to military operations is ensuring that military commanders receive timely information required to successfully execute their combat missions, while minimizing the loss of American lives. The U.S. intelligence community (IC) provides the military with a wide array of support, ranging from an encyclopedia of basic information on military forces, logistics, climate, and terrain, to precise targeting information and battle damage assessments (BDA). In support of long-term planning, the IC provides the U.S. military with assessments based on all-source analyses on future force dispositions, capabilities, and intentions of foreign militaries. The IC also assesses the capabilities of current and anticipated weapon systems of potential opponents. Such information is needed to prevent technological surprise and to ensure the technological superiority of U.S. military equipment.

The headquarters of the U.S. Central Intelligence Agency at Langley, Virginia

THE FBI

The headquarters of the Federal Bureau of Investigation (FBI) in Washington, D.C.

The Federal Bureau of Investigation (FBI) exists to protect and defend the United States against terrorist and foreign intelligence threats, to uphold and enforce the criminal laws of the United States, and to provide leadership and criminal justice services to federal, state, municipal, and international agencies and partners.

The FBI's main priorities are to:
1. Protect the United States from terrorist attack;
2. Protect the United States against foreign intelligence operations and espionage;
3. Protect the United States against cyber-based attacks and high-technology crimes;
4. Combat public corruption at all levels;
5. Protect civil rights;
6. Combat transnational/national criminal organizations and enterprises;
7. Combat major white-collar crime;
8. Combat significant violent crime;
9. Support federal, state, local and international partners;
10. Upgrade technology to successfully perform the FBI's mission.

THE FBI'S MOST WANTED

These were the FBI's most wanted terrorists at the start of 2008. The figures in brackets are the FBI's offered rewards for information leading directly to the apprehension or conviction of each individual:

Osama bin Laden ($25 million)
Ayman Al-Zawahiri ($25 million)
Abdelkarim Hussein Mohamed Al-Nasser ($5 million)
Abdullah Ahmed Abdullah ($5 million)
Ali Atwa ($5 million)
Ramadan Abdullah Mohammad Shallah ($5 million)
Isnilon Totoni Hapilon ($5 million)
Jamel Ahmed Mohammed Ali Al-Badawi ($5 million)
Anas Al-Liby ($5 million)
Hasan Izz-Al-Din ($5 million)
Ahmed Mohammed Hamed Ali ($5 million)
Fazul Abdullah Mohammed ($5 million)
Sheikh Ahmed Salim Swedan ($5 million)
Abd Al Aziz Awda ($5 million)
Jaber A. Elbaneh ($5 million)
Abdul Rahman Yasin ($5 million)
Fahid Msalam ($5 million)
Ahmad Ibrahim Al-Mughassil ($5 million)
Ali Saed Bin Ali El-Hoorie ($5 million)
Saif Al-Adel ($5 million)
Ibrahim Salih Mohammed Al-Yacoub ($5 million)
Mohammed Ali Hamadei ($5 million)
Adam Yahiye Gadahn ($1 million)

The FBI has a total of 31,244 employees. This figure includes 12,851 special agents and 18,393 support professionals, such as intelligence analysts, language specialists, scientists, information technology specialists, and others.

The National Security Branch (NSB) was established on December 9, 2005, in response to a presidential directive to establish a national security service that combines the missions, capabilities, and resources of the counterterrorism, counterintelligence, and intelligence elements of the FBI under the leadership of a senior FBI official. In July 2006, the Weapons of Mass Destruction Directorate was created within the NSB to integrate WMD components previously spread throughout the FBI. The NSB also includes the Terrorist Screening Center.

After the September 11, 2001, attacks on the World Trade Center and the Pentagon, Washington was flooded with expressions of sympathy from world leaders. The Bush Administration worked to turn these words into an international "coalition of the willing" against terrorism. Some of the countries who offered full military support in 2001 were: **Canada** (six naval ships, aircraft, special operations forces, and 2,000 military personnel); **Germany** (up to 3,900 troops; surveillance planes and crews); **Italy** (2,700 troops) **Israel** (troops and weapons); **Turkey** (90-man special forces unit); **Philippines** (the use of two military bases); **Australia** (1,500 troops, aircraft, and naval vessels); **Britain** (a naval group, troops, and fighter and transport aircraft).

Even countries that were traditionally hostile to the United States condemned the 9/11 attacks. North Korea, for example, a country long isolated and a traditional foe of the United States since the 1950s, called the attacks "shocking" and "very regretful." Iran condemned the attacks and urged the United Nations to lead an international fight against terrorism. It also said, however, that U.S. planes could not use its airspace for possible retaliatory strikes.

The North Atlantic Treaty Organization (NATO) consists of 26 states. It exists to ensure the security of its members. After the attacks of September 11, 2001, NATO invoked Article 5 of its treaty to support the war on terror. The article states: "An armed attack against one or more of them in Europe or North America shall be considered an attack against them all and consequently they agree that, if such an armed attack occurs, each of them will assist the Party or Parties so attacked by taking forthwith, individually and in concert with the other Parties, such action as it deems necessary, including the use of armed force."

NATO members condemned the terrorist attacks and all offered their support to the United States, pledging to "undertake all efforts to combat the scourge of terrorism." This was followed by declarations of solidarity and support from Russia and Ukraine. Since 2001, NATO forces have been deployed to Afghanistan to combat terrorism.

Canadian armored vehicles in Afghanistan—part of the NATO effort to combat the Taliban and al Qaeda in the country.

MEMBERS OF THE COALITION

Members of the coalition in 2008:

Afghanistan	Hungary	Portugal
Albania	Iceland	Romania
Angola	Italy	Rwanda
Australia	Japan	Singapore
Azerbaijan	Kuwait	Slovakia
Bulgaria	Latvia	Solomon Islands
Colombia	Lithuania	South Korea
Costa Rica	Macedonia	Spain
Czech Republic	Marshall Islands	Tonga
Denmark	Micronesia	Turkey
Dominican Republic	Mongolia	Uganda
El Salvador	Netherlands	Ukraine
Eritrea	Nicaragua	United Kingdom
Estonia	Palau	United States
Ethiopia	Panama	Uzbekistan
Georgia	Philippines	
Honduras	Poland	

NATO IN AFGHANISTAN

NATO is a key component of the international community's engagement in Afghanistan, assisting the Afghan authorities in providing security and stability, paving the way for reconstruction and effective governance. Through the UN-mandated International Security Assistance Force (ISAF), NATO is assisting the Afghan government in extending and exercising its authority and influence across the country, creating the conditions for stabilization and reconstruction.

On October 5, 2006, in another landmark step for NATO, NATO-ISAF took command of the international military forces in eastern Afghanistan from the U.S.-led Coalition. NATO's mission now covers the whole of Afghanistan where it has command of some 50,700 troops (including National Support Elements) from 41 countries and 26 Provincial Reconstruction Teams (PRTs). This is NATO's first and largest ground operation outside Europe.

THE UNITED NATIONS

The United Nations (UN) is an organization that exists to promote world peace and security. It currently has a membership of 192 states and its headquarters are in New York City in the United States. One of the most important UN bodies is the Security Council, which has the authority to send military forces to troublespots around the world.

The Security Council has 15 members. Five of these are permanent members and the General Assembly elects 10 other members for two-year terms. The five permanent members of the Security Council are China, France, the Russian Federation, the United Kingdom, and the United States.

The comparative advantages of the United Nations are its universal membership, its political legitimacy (it is the world's only forum for building, consolidating, and using power on behalf of the international community), impartiality, technical expertise, and ability to convene and mobilize power. Its comparative disadvantages are its lengthy decision-making processes, high cost structure, insufficient resources, and bureaucratic rigidity.

After the World Trade Center attacks of September 11, 2001, the UN passed Security Council Resolutions 1373 and 1390, adopted September 28, 2001, and January 16, 2002, respectively. These resolutions required all UN member states to: "Freeze without

delay the funds and other financial assets or economic resources" of those individuals and entities designated by the United Nations as belonging to, or associated with, the Taliban or al Qaeda.

The United Nations (UN) headquarters in New York City, where 192 member states can debate world issues, including terrorism.

AFGHANISTAN

In late 2001, the UN Security Council authorized the United States to overthrow the Taliban government in Afghanistan, as an offensive against the terrorist al Qaeda organization. In March 2002, the Council established the UN Assistance Mission for Afghanistan (UNAMA) to manage all UN humanitarian, relief, recovery, and reconstruction activities. The Taliban enjoyed an upsurge of military success in 2007-2008 and several NATO countries have expressed concern about the political viability of the operation. Public support for deployments to Afghanistan in countries such as Germany and Canada has evaporated. The media have reported on U.S.-UK air bombardment of innocent civilians, as well as bold Taliban attacks against U.S. and NATO forces, suggesting that the UN intervention is failing to produce the promised security, democracy, and prosperity.

A U.S. soldier on guard duty outside Camp Delta, part of the U.S. detention center at Guantanamo Bay, Cuba.

The Guantanamo Bay Detention Camp is a military prison of the United States of America situated on the southeastern tip of the island of Cuba. In this prison, suspected terrorists are held indefinitely without charge or trial. It was established in 2002, after the World Trade Center attacks, as a holding facility for people deemed "enemy combatants." This could include U.S. citizens or residents, and was primarily meant to hold anyone suspected of terrorism. The various prison camps, of which there are several, have also held individuals from Afghanistan and other countries who are supposed to have links to al Qaeda, the Taliban, and other Islamic terrorist organizations. At one point, the camp held 700 inmates, but by 2009 there were around 270 detainees, of whom 100 were Yemenis.

CLOSING THE BASE?

In 2008 a U.S. Supreme Court decision granted detainees at Guantanamo the right to challenge their detention in civilian courts, meaning that federal judges have the power to check the U.S. government's assertion that the 270 people still held there are dangerous terrorists. That will force officials to answer questions about evidence that they have long deflected. Detainees' lawyers had long said that the government would not be able to justify the detention of many held there. Pentagon officials, on the other hand, maintained that classified evidence established that many of them are dangerous. The federal courts now have the power to sort through those claims. President Barack Obama, who entered office in January 2009, stated that the base will be closed.

At the end of 2008, the global situation in the ongoing War on Terror looked as follows:

Iraq

Terror network Al Qaeda had been driven out of its erstwhile strongholds in Anbar, Baghdad, and Diyala provinces. Its last refuge was in the northern city of Mosul, but even there it was under Iraqi–U.S. attack. From Basra to Baghdad, Shi'a terrorists who were loosely affiliated with Moqtada al-Sadr's Mahdi army were also in retreat, thanks primarily to the operations of the Iraqi security forces.

Afghanistan

Al Qaeda was still reeling from the blows it suffered in the aftermath of 9/11 when nearly 80 percent of its members in Afghanistan were killed in 2001. Since then, more have been killed or captured in countries ranging from Yemen and Pakistan to Spain and Indonesia.

Outside of Iraq and Afghanistan

Al Qaeda has not managed to mount any major attacks on any U.S. target, much less on the U.S. homeland, since 9/11. With a few exceptions —such as the bombings in Bali (2002), Madrid (2004), and London (2005)—the attacks staged by al Qaeda and its affiliates have mostly killed fellow Muslims. This has led to a major backlash in the Muslim world. In Pakistan, support for Islamist political parties has collapsed— dropping by more than four-fifths between the 2002 and 2008 national elections. And in the Northwest Frontier Province, where al Qaeda has its strongest presence in Pakistan, support for Osama bin Laden dropped from 70 percent in August 2007 to 4 percent in January 2008.

The human cost of the War on Terror has been high. To the end of 2008 the United States has suffered more than 72,000 battlefield casualties since 2001: 4,372 U.S. soldiers have died and another 67,671 have been wounded in action, injured in accidents, or died from illness in Iraq and Afghanistan. To these must be added the more than 100,000 Iraqi and 7,000 Afghan civilian deaths since the beginning of the War on Terror.

FURTHER RESOURCES

PUBLICATIONS

Bobbitt, Philip, *Terror and Consent: The Wars for the Twenty-First Century*, Knopf, New York, 2008.

Burke, Jason, *Al-Qaeda: The True Story of Radical Islam*, I. B. Tauris, London, 2004.

Cassidy, Robert, *Counterinsurgency and the Global War on Terror*, Stanford University Press, Palo Alto, CA, 2008.

Chossudovsky, Michel, *America's "War on Terrorism"*, Global Research, Montreal, Qc, 2005.

Clarke, Richard A., *Against All Enemies: Inside America's War on Terror*, Simon & Schuster, New York, 2004.

Coker, Christopher, *The Warrior Ethos: Military Culture and the War on Terror*, Routledge, New York, 2007.

Corum, James S., *Fighting the War on Terror: A Counterinsurgency Strategy*, Zenith Press, St. Paul, MN, 2007.

Croft, Stuart, *Culture, Crisis and America's War on Terror*, Cambridge University Press, Cambridge, 2006.

Davis, Todd A., *The Global War On Terror*, Xlibris Corporation, Philadelphia, PA, 2008.

Esposito, John L., *Unholy War: Terror in the Name of Islam*, Oxford University Press, New York, 2003.

Feaman, Peter, *Wake Up, America!*, Woodmont Publishers, Liberty Corner, NJ, 2007.

Gabriel, Mark A., *Journey into the Mind of an Islamic Terrorist*, Strang Communications, Lake Mary, FL, 2006.

Habeck, Mary, *Knowing the Enemy: Jihadist Ideology and the War on Terror*, Yale University Press, London, 2007.

Halliday, Fred, *Two Hours that Shook the World: September 11 2001: Causes and Consequences*, Palgrave, New York, 2002.

Hewitt, Steve, *The British War on Terror: Terrorism and Counter-Terrorism on the Home Front Since 9/11*, Continuum, New York, 2008.

Hiro, Dilip, *War Without End: The Rise of Islamist Terrorism and the Global Response*, Routledge, New York, 2002.

Hoge, James F., *Understanding the War on Terror*, Foreign Affairs, Palm Coast, FL, 2005.

Ibrahim, Raymond, *The Al Qaeda Reader*, Broadway, New York, 2007.

Ivie, Robert L., *Democracy and America's War on Terror*, University of Alabama Press, Tuscaloosa, AL, 2006.

Jacobson, Sid, and Colon, Ernie, *After 9/11: America's War on Terror (2001–)*, Hill and Wang, New York, 2008.

Jacquard, Roland, *In the Name of Osama Bin Laden: Global Terrorism and the Bin Laden Brotherhood*, Duke University Press, Durham, NC, 2002.

Lewis, Bernard, *The Crisis of Islam: Holy War and Unholy Terror*, Modern Library, New York, 2005.

Lustick, Ian S., *Trapped in the War on Terror*, University of Pennsylvania Press, Philadelphia, PA, 2006.

Mead, Walter Russell *Power, Terror, Peace, and War: America's Grand Strategy in a World at Risk*, Vintage, New York, 2005.

Riedel, Bruce, *The Search for al Qaeda: Its Leadership, Ideology, and Future*, Brookings Institution Press, Washington, D.C., 2008.

Rubin, Barry, and Rubin, Judith Colp, *Anti-American Terrorism and the Middle East: Understanding the Violence*, Oxford University Press, New York, 2002.

Schultheis, Rob, *Hunting bin Laden: How al-Qaeda Is Winning the War on Terror*, Skyhorse Publishing, New York, 2008.

Stevens, Anthony, *Roots of War and Terror*, Continuum, New York, 2005.

Telhami, Shibley, *Identity and Foreign Policy in the Middle East*, Cornell University Press, Ithaca, NY, 2002.

Telhami, Shibley, *The Stakes: America and the Middle East*, Westview Press, New York, 2002.

Wright, Lawrence, *The Looming Tower: Al-Qaeda and the Road to 9/11*, Knopf, New York, 2006.

WEBSITES

http://news.bbc.co.uk/1/hi/in_depth/world/2001/war_on_terror/
BBC special report on the War on Terror.

www.cnn.com/SPECIALS/2001/trade.center/
War on Terror news, analysis, commentary, interactives, photos, video, audio, and web resources.

www.lib.umich.edu/govdocs/usterror.html
Directory covering the September 11th attack, previous and post attacks, counterterrorism, and terrorism in and from other countries.

www.iwar.org.uk/homesec/resources/war-on-terror/timeline
Timeline of the War on Terror.

www.dhs.gov
Official site of the U.S. Department of Homeland Security.

www.nato.int/isaf/
Official site of NATO's International Security Assistance Force in Afghanistan.

INDEX